Edible and Poisonous Plants of Northern California

Text and Illustrations by

James Wiltens

WILDERNESS PRESS
BERKELEY

WARNING

The Publisher and the Author disclaim any liability for injury that may result from following the instructions for collecting, preparing or consuming plants described in this guide. Efforts have been taken to assure the field drawings and descriptions of plants represented in the illustrations are accurate representations of the genus and species noted. **It should be understood that growth conditions, improper identification, and varietal differences (not recognized as yet in scientific literature), as well as an individual's own sensitivity or allergic response can contribute to a hazard in sampling a new plant food.**

Previously published as *Plants Your Mother Never Told You About*, and *Thistle Greens and Mistletoe*

Library of Congress Card Catalog Number pending
ISBN 0-89997-249-7

Manufactured in the United States of America
Published by **Wilderness Press**
2440 Bancroft Way
Berkeley, CA 94704
(800) 443-7227, FAX (510) 548-1355
mail@wildernesspress.com

Contact us for a free catalog
Visit our web site at **www.wildernesspress.com**

ACKNOWLEDGEMENTS

I want to thank my brother, Roy, who was reasonably easily coerced into again helping his big brother on yet another strange project. Though he must admit, doing typesetting and printing is easier than working on the gold dredge many summers ago.

My mother for the infallible dictionary in her head and her nagging insistence on appropriate English grammar (which if there are any errors, are due to my own stubborn perversity at not always following the rules).

To Janet for her patience and half-nelson approach in wrenching me away from the writer's neanderthal use of a pencil to word processing "computerese".

And to Russell, for the use of his library and as a sounding board.

DEDICATION

This book is dedicated to the first prehistoric man who had the courage to stick an unknown plant into his mouth. His first words would probably have been interpreted, "one small bite for a man, one giant gobble for mankind." Or something to that effect.

TABLE OF CONTENTS

page

III. POISONOUS PLANTS

A PRIMITIVE IN SUBURBIA

Silicon Valley is my home for 6 months a year. Every Fall I make a sabbatical from the high mountains of the Sierra to this technological Disneyland, bristling with man-made marvels and the artifacts of genius. As the months pass, insulated by concrete, foam and chrome, I begin to sense an isolation. The primitive in me wants some release, an alternate lifestyle if only for a weekend. Foraging is my time machine, a way of satisfying that bit of primitive psyche, a liberation from the awesome dependency I attribute to technology.

I eat weeds. Not a poetic description — but quite succinct. In a society where maternal supermarkets, ubiquitous 7-11's, and fast-food franchises play Big Brother to our intestinal needs — I am on a primitive food quest, an attempt to re-establish my link to the source. It's a declaration of independence in an increasingly technology dependent world. Such a quest is an amazing revelation.

The plants that nourished our ancestors are growing all around us. Imagine finding a produce section in every vacant lot: acorn bread from oak nuts, a salad of purslane garnished with wild radish pods and mustard leaves, curly dock pie topped with mint leaves and sections of prickly pear from a cactus. At a time when that dowager, agribusiness, demands monetary fidelity, there is still an opportunity to flirt with winsome mother nature. Such a fling is food for the soul.

During the summer I teach at Deer Crossing Wilderness Camp located in the High Sierra. In our mountain setting my students don't become too concerned when I drop down on all fours and ferret among the meadow grass in search of edible plants. The setting seems appropriate for an "altered state," but when I pursue my hobby in a vacant lot sandwiched between IBM and a housing development, it does raise some eyebrows. In such cases, I find the urban thought process responds better to, "I'm conducting an environmental impact study" rather than "Oh, just looking for dinner."

My field trips have become a treasure hunt full of the thrill of discovery. For me it has become a game, a pastime and an avocation — a natural scavenger hunt on a grand scale. As I find each new plant I gain a literacy that was natural to primitive man, the ability to read the landscape in terms of basic needs. There is a satisfaction and an excitement in this rediscovery which makes me feel a oneness with the natural world.

CHEAP THRILLS

A burgeois attitude towards free food is not an affectation of the modern age. In 1854, Thoreau wrote "...yet men have come to such a pass that they frequently starve, not for want of necessities but for want of luxuries." He wrote these words after a meal of wild purslane.

Unless a food is couched in grandiose verbiage or given an aura of sophistication, usually monetarily related, we have a tendency to view it with high-nosed disdain. How ridiculous. Our stomachs still process the protein, carbohydrates and fibers in the same manner–regardless of price or pretension. Wild foods are neither humble nor less pedigreed than their farm-propagated cousins.

A serious forager can make a dent in the grocery bill. In East San Jose there are enclaves of recent immigrants, people who only recently have broken their ties with the land. In these areas you will notice a marked reduction of greenery in vacant lots. Stir-fried, baked and boiled, nature's free bounty contributes to the diet of these transplanted people. Wild foods can supplement or replace a number of the vegetables, fruits and grains purchased at the supermarket.

As I have learned to recognize edible plants, I am amazed at the mass and diversity that surround us even in an urban environment. Empty lots, watersheds, open spaces, parks, creekbeds and the neighbor's lawn will provide you dinner. Of course this requires a commitment of some energy and, for most, the money saved is not the impelling motive for foraging.

TOWARDS A NATURAL AWARENESS

For some reason, whenever man sticks something in his mouth he develops a keen interest. The plant that most people would never recognize, the forager knows intimately. Edible plants take on a high profile. They become reference points in the natural world. Like old friends they welcome you to the out-of-doors. And as you become acquainted with your first plants you will be encouraged to learn even more about their environment.

CULINARY ESCAPISM

Most people are food conformists. Think how we bow to the conglomerate dictates of food conformity. How can you be a wild and crazy guy if you're always sipping those bland vanilla and cellulose shakes. If for no other reason, surprise your palate, assert your prerogative as a stomach with individual tastes. The gourmet can find some excitement in preparing interesting and tasty dishes from fascinating new ingredients.

NUTRITIONAL ISSUES

Many undomesticated plants have high nutritional value. The well-known dandelion rates higher in protein, carbohydrates, vitamin C and A than its relative, lettuce. In some cases, because wild plants grow without benefit of herbicides, pesticides, minimum spacing and other agribusiness techniques of forcing growth, weeds may have a higher nutritional value and fewer chemical drawbacks than some supermarket produce.

SUBURBAN SURVIVAL

Most edible plant books will point out the survival benefit of learning to forage. If your passenger plane should be forced down in the Yukon Delta or Hindu Kush you will have a better chance of surviving. Obviously such disasters are of negligible concern to most people.

But...have you ever thought how dependent we have become on the technological marvels that pump food into the Bay Area? A small tourniquet applied to our highway system and food stores would be depleted within days. Should the San Andreas Fault do a little hard rock and roll, modern man's food arteries may just dry up. Your wild plant knowledge could be that far-fetched insurance policy that contributes to survival.

HOW ARE YOU GOING TO LEARN?

Foraging is an experiential activity. What is gleaned from the flat pages of a book must be transformed into a 3 dimensional reality.

Make it a game. You can compete with yourself or others. Look thru this book the evening before you go foraging. You don't need to memorize, just get a feeling for what the plants look like. Then take the book and go to an open area and start searching. When you see something that jogs your memory, look for the appropriate drawing. If the plant checks with the illustration and description then write it down on your list – like a scavenger hunt. In no time at all you will be recognizing a variety of plants. If you are competing with someone, then set a time limit and compare your lists at the end. You can then go back and check each other which will further reinforce your memory.

If you wish to accelerate your learning or go into more depth, consider the following:

★ Going out with knowledgeable people (California Native Plant Society).

★ Take a botany class concerned with the native flora. A valuable skill which is best learned in an academic setting is how to use a key. Keys, such as Munz's "A California Flora," give scientifically accurate descriptions of many plants native to California. Unfortunately, the layman may find a key somewhat confusing without knowledgeable assistance.

★ Visit a botanical garden where the plants are clearly labeled. U.C. Berkeley has an excellent botanical garden, one section is even set aside for plants utilized by California Indians (location: Tilden Park Drive, for information, write, Regional Parks Botanic Garden, Tilden Regional Park, Berkeley, CA 94708).

  U.C. Santa Cruz also maintains an arboretum, but not as extensive as the one in Berkeley.

★ Many regional parks have nature trails where the native flora has been identified by numbered posts. One site is Joaquin Miller park in Oakland (Chinquapin Nature Trail). Another is the Uvas Canyon Park in Santa Clara County.

★ Sunset Magazine in Menlo Park maintains a garden of plants native to the Pacific Coastal States. For information on visiting the garden, call (415) 321-3600.

★ Read more books on the subject. A bibliography at the end will suggest additional reading material.

Once you have made positive identification of a plant, try it in a recipe. As a precaution, and due to different individuals' sensitivities to food, **when trying a new plant for the first time, eat only a small quantity.**

WHEN TRYING A WILD PLANT FOR THE FIRST TIME, CONSUME A SMALL QUANTITY.

A ROSE BY ANY OTHER NAME

How a plant is named is critically important. There are two ways of identifying a plant. One is to give it a **common name**, such as oak, dandelion or miner's lettuce. This is the manner in which we identify plants in our everyday language. The problem is that common names are variable. From one section of the country to another, different names may be applied to the same plant. This can be confusing as I learned when talking to someone from a different state. A young lady asked me if I had eaten the leaves from 'blowballs'. I told her that the plant did not sound familiar. She seemed surprised that an avid forager did not know what blowballs were. Not wanting to appear unknowledgeable to such an attractive young woman, I assumed a scholarly look and asked her to describe the plant. Part way through her description I realized the plant she was talking about was the ordinary dandelion. Blowballs was just another common name for dandelion, or from her view point, dandelion was just another common name for blowballs.

The danger inherent in relying on common names is the possibility of confusion - confusion which could lead to death. For instance, there is a tree known as hemlock which is reputed to be edible, yet there is also a violently poisonous weed which goes by the same name. Another example would be a trailing vine referred to as wild cucumber, unfortunately it is in a totally different genus from the cultured cucumbers, in fact it is considered toxic.

There are some plants that have 5 or 6 common names. In some cases, different common names may be used interchangeably – by the same person. The possibility for error and confusion when using common names was recognized a long time ago. In the early written histories of useful plants (their books were called herbals) there were often

COMMON NAMES CAN BE CONFUSING.

conflicting common names. Scientists, cooks, pharmacists and physicians were in a quagmire when it came to common names, since everyone seemed to have their favorite name for a plant. The only way to be sure if they were talking about the same thing was to have the plant right in front of them so there could be agreement.

Then came the Age of Reason.

A Swedish physician, Linnaeus, came up with a scientific method of nomenclature. Plants were classified by certain features and divided into natural categories. The divisions consisted of Plant kingdom, phylum, class, order, family, **genus** and **species**. Each individual plant was given a genus name and a species name, which are used only for that particular plant. For instance, the common dandelion has the genus name *Taraxacum* and the species name, *officinale*. Genus and species names can be likened to people's names. Your last name would be equivalent to genus and your first name would represent species, Smith (genus) and Jim (species). The scientific name is by far the most reliable way of describing a plant.

There are certain conventions in scientific nomenclature that you should understand. In a previous example, I mentioned that the dandelion is technically *Taraxacum officinale*. For the sake of brevity, if the full technical name has been applied to a plant, subsequent written references to the plant will be abbreviated to *T. officinale*. In addition, if you see the genus name followed by the letters 'sps.' it refers to species in that genus. As an example, *Typha sps.* refers to the ten or so species in the cat-tail genus.

This book lists both the common names applied to a plant as well as the scientific name. In many situations the common name is more comfortable to use, but **where accuracy is concerned you must use scientific nomenclature.**

FOOD PREJUDICE

Many of our tastes are acquired due to our cultural origins. It's hard to imagine that some foods, so popular today, were once thought to be rather innocuous. In the 1600's one author describes the tomato as "...yielding very little nourishment and [they are] naught and corrupt." I take it the author did not like tomatoes. I know that yogurt, squash and spinach did not rank high on my list of preferred foods until I established a taste for them. If you have been 'MacDonaldized', conditioned to salivate at the sight of the Big "M", the appreciation of some wild foods may take a little time.

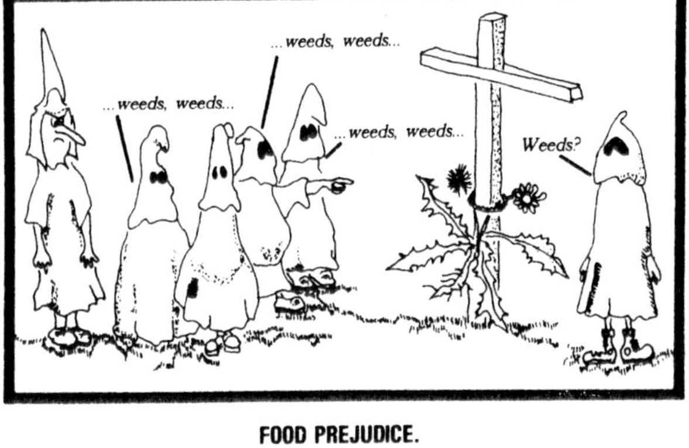

FOOD PREJUDICE.

To give wild plants a fair chance at appreciation, they must be picked at the right stage. If your first adventure with a plant leaves a 'sour taste' in your mouth, maybe it has been picked at an inappropriate time. Green tomatoes, unripe bananas, mushy apples, wilted lettuce and petrified radishes could make carnivores of us all. But we are educated about these foods and know when a plant product is ripe. In general, many of the greens described in this book are best picked young.

MANY PLANTS ARE BEST PICKED YOUNG.

PILLAGING IS A NO–NO

When foraging, your purpose is not to mimic Attila the Hun by raping and pillaging the countryside. Take reasonable amounts of plants. If the plants are rare then leave them alone.

That does it!
No more foraging
with Arnold.

TAKE ONLY WHAT YOU NEED.

The early Indians had a reverential attitude toward some important food crops. When harvesting prickly pear (*Opuntia* sps.), they would pluck out a hair as an offering to the gods. I imagine that such a practice, if re-instituted today, would curtail excessive foraging.

Rather than plucking a hair, I show my thankfulness by practicing some simple environmental guidelines. If a plant is not particularly abundant, I spread some seeds to encourage the species growth. I may even go so far as to scratch the ground a bit and cover the seeds. I also find it unnecessary to excavate the entire root system of a plant when all I really need are the leaves. Many plants will grow back if the root crown is left intact. Such simple practices go a long way to helping preserve a free harvest.

BOO BOOS – WAY BACK WHEN

Modern man owes his primitive ancestors a great deal. Our knowledge about plants is largely based on brave (or very hungry) human guinea pigs. The primitive nutrition laboratory probably consisted of one low brow researcher with limited testing equipment, his stomach. The results were tabulated in a simple manner – "taste good", "taste bad", "make Ug sick" or "inconclusive results due to dead researcher". Since much of this information was passed down by word of mouth, there cropped up some errors. The tenacity of these errors, even into our own modern scientific age, is fascinating. Why man preserves what seems so clearly erroneous to the trained mind goes beyond reason. It is probably an innate desire to find a simple way to handle a complex problem.

The early herbals were notoriously inaccurate in applying traits to the plants they described. The authors of these early works were often writing on hearsay and in many cases had never even seen the plant they were writing about. The writers of some herbals would go into paroxysms of ecstasy as they described a plant which was good for salads, capable of curing blindness, an aid to the fair sex in removing weight, known to staunch the flow of blood, purify the liver and drive werewolves from your door. Drive werewolves from your door – that I'm willing to accept, but all the other medicine show talk I view with a jaundiced eye. The reason I mention this is that some modern day authors still quote from 16th and 17th century herbals to prove their claims about the miraculous properties of certain plants.

Some plants do have medicinal claims, but there are probably an equal number that have proven false. The flash-in-the-pan miracle plant is questionable. Consistent nutrition utilizing nature's bounty is the most reasonable claim.

OLD WIVES TALES

Some common wives tales that have caused poisoning and death in humans are the following:

1. **If the plant shows signs of having been eaten by an animal then it is O.K. for human consumption.** This is a common misconception. How do you know that some squirrel has not nibbled on a particular plant to commit suicide?

Go ahead Fred I'm sure it's O.K.
I just saw a human eat some

JUST BECAUSE A PLANT SHOWS SIGNS OF HAVING BEEN CONSUMED BY AN ANIMAL, DOES NOT MEAN IT IS SAFE FOR HUMAN CONSUMPTION.

In the name of science, many animals have been provided toxic forage plants. The animals often eat large quantities of these plants before expiring. This is particularly true if the plant has no immediately unappetizing taste to the animal.

There are also cases in which an animal's digestive system seems able to handle what would be toxic to man. Birds can often be seen nibbling mistletoe berries and goats show no ill effects from eating poison oak, yet if man were to consume either of these plants he would be in serious trouble.

2. **Just a little taste is O.K.** is another common misconception. There are a number of plant toxins where just a little is too much. A single seed of castor bean (*Ricinus communis*) can kill a child, a single seed from rosary pea (*Abrus precatorius*) can kill an adult, a single leaf of oleander (*Nerium oleander*) is capable of causing death and water hemlock (*Cicuta maculata*) root the size of a walnut can kill a cow. You should never try a nibble of any plant unless you know what it is and can vouch for its safety.

3. **Some people will tell you, boiling a plant will destroy the poisonous principle.** This is one of those wives' tales that is half true. There are some plants that will be rendered safe after boiling, but there are also a number of plants that will remain toxic. The Indians of Delaware would commit suicide by boiling mountain laurel leaves (*Kalmia sps.*) into a tea. Sometimes I wonder if they were knowingly committing suicide. Maybe they were just following some old wives tale that said boiling would make it safe.

4. It is a good idea to view any broad sweeping claim or test with suspicion. There is the story of a family from Vietnam that had recently moved to the Santa Clara Valley. They had been told that you can tell the difference between toxic and edible mushrooms by putting a silver coin in boiling water with several mushrooms. If the coin tarnishes, then the mushrooms are poisonous. If the coin remains shiny - bon appetit. This wives' tale cost the family dearly. Several family members died after eating a toxic species of mushroom which had passed "the test".

If the plant is going in your mouth, take great pains to separate fact from fiction. If you don't, the fact and fiction may separate in your stomach and give you great pain in the process.

I'M ALMOST CERTAIN

Conviction is a wonderful quality, but, when foraging it had better be backed up with knowledge. Before eating a plant you must be certain of its identification, because once you commit - open the lips, over the gums, look out stomach, here it comes.

ALWAYS BE CERTAIN OF A PLANT'S IDENTITY.

When meeting a new plant for the first time, I always check it out with at least 3 field guides. I never "assume" that it is the correct plant. Make an effort to check the descriptions and diagrams. This is a critical habit to establish early in your career. Since there is the possibility of becoming quite intimate, get in the habit of not accepting blind dates with an unknown plant.

When teaching classes in wilderness survival, I am always cautious about what plants I introduce my students to. For beginners I avoid making introductions of edible species that have look-a-like poisonous cousins. In the early stages it's important to stick with plants that are distinctive and not easily confused. That effort has been made in this guide.

Even when you know a plant fairly well, different growth conditions (ie., sun, water, soil) can make dramatic changes in appearance. The plant that is normally a bush when growing on hardpan dirt is a large tree in rich alluvial soil, the petite leaves in shade are as big as your hand in the sun and what normally bears several berries is covered with fruit during a wet year. The original characteristics are still there, but it's like looking in a funny house mirror, things are seemingly out of proportion.

GROWTH CONDITIONS CAN AFFECT A PLANT'S APPEARANCE.

ROSES ARE EDIBLE, VIOLETS ARE BLUE, NIGHTSHADE IS DEADLY, SO YOU BETTER KNOW IT TOO!

They'll pollute your blood, knock out your eyeballs, fibrillate your heart-pump, deflate your lungs, and give you visions of angels. There are nasty plants out there. Plants that contain alkaloids, glucosides, heavy metals, hallucinogens - enough poison to bring a smile to Lucretia Borgia's lips (a woman of Italian nobility who had a chemical solution to matters of inheritance).

In foraging it's important to know some of the villains. In one section of this book I have grouped the edible and useful plants and in another section I have grouped poisonous plants that every forager should know. A knowledge of standard poisonous plants and their effects has the added advantage of making you less hasty to nibble an unknown plant.

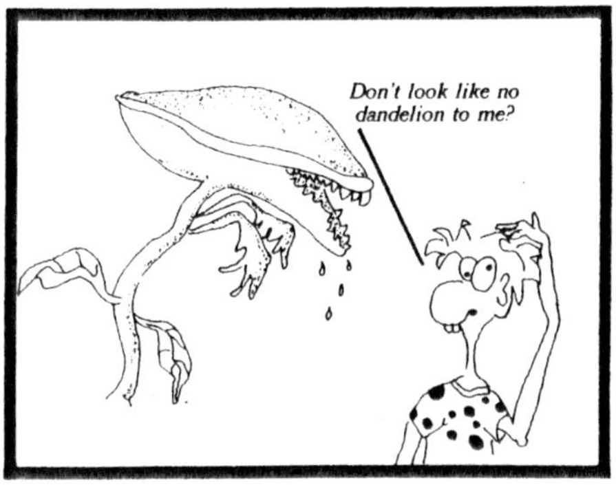

KNOWING SOME OF THE DEADLY PLANTS CAN HELP TO AVOID SERIOUS MISTAKES.

It is important to understand that some plants, normally considered safe, can be toxic under certain growing conditions:

1. **Never collect plants within fifty feet of a busy roadway.** It has been found that plants can concentrate toxic by-products of automobile exhaust. High concentrations of lead have been found in some roadway plants.

PLANTS GROWING NEAR A ROAD SHOULD BE CONSIDERED UNSAFE TO EAT.

2. **If you suspect that soil has been contaminated with poison, then avoid foraging in that area.** Some plants can transport high concentrations of heavy metals or other poisonous constituents into their tissue. High levels of such substances as selenium, arsenic and nitrates have been found in dangerous amounts in plants normally considered safe.

3. **Avoid collecting plants in areas that have been sprayed with pesticides or herbicides.** Your neighbor's rose bushes may contain many ripe rose hips for use in a herbal tea, but if the plants have been misted with malathion then make the sign of the cross and pass them by.

   The county often takes on local weed patches by spraying herbicides. If the plants are dampened with a black or oily film, or if there are strange discolored spots on the plant then there is a chance that poisons have been used.

   Another signal that pesticides may have been used in an area is the presence of yellow dead plants right next to healthy green ones.

WHERE ARE THE MUSHROOMS?

You may wonder why a book on foraging contains no information on mushrooms. I have deleted mushrooms for the following reasons: mushrooms, in general, have minimal food value, they are somewhat difficult for the beginner to identify, and deadly mushrooms contain some of the most violent toxins known.

While obtaining my degree in Botany, I took a mushroom course from a world-recognized mycologist at U.C. Berkeley. I assumed, that with his knowledge, he went out collecting mushrooms for gourmet purposes. I was quite surprised when he explained to me that he did not eat wild mushrooms. The inherent risks and the possibility of different individual susceptibility to mushroom toxins were his reasons for abstaining. This revelation has always dampened my enthusiasm for collecting mushrooms.

WILD MUSHROOMS ARE BEST LEFT TO THE EXPERTS.

AGAVE

Agave americana
(Agave Family: Agavaceae)

OTHER NAMES: Century Plant, Mescal, American Aloe (not a true Aloe)

DESCRIPTION: This plant is a gigantic rosette of thick succulent leaves. Leaves may be as much as 6 feet long. A row of sturdy spines progresses up the edge of each leaf and finishes with a wicked spike at the tip of the leaf. Blue-green in color. Contrary to popular belief, Agave flowers much more often than every 100 years. With sufficient water the plant sends up a flower shoot in 10-15 years. The flower stalk, which looks like a giant asparagus, may rise as high as 20 feet.

HABITAT: Dry soil, hillsides, desert environment. Often planted as an ornamental in rock gardens.

CAUTION: ***The spines pose an obvious hazard. The fresh juice is also a possible problem, it can cause a rash in sensitive people that is comparable to poison oak.***

Unknowingly, I tested my sensitivity to the plant when younger. Agave contains a fiber that can be used to make rope. Using my bare hands, I would strip these threads from the plant to work into fishing line. Though I am sensitive to poison oak, I never experienced any skin problems with Agave.

Sources have informed me that raw Agave is poisonous. Even a small bite can burn the mouth. I am willing to take their word for this.

USES: Indians of the Southwest used a number of Agave species as food sources (*A. utahensis, A. deserti* and *A. shawii*). The plants can be used at any time, but are reputed to be best when the flowering stalk is just beginning to rise from the center. Use a machete to remove the outer perimeter of leaves from the plant. Then ram a shovel into the base of the plant and pry it free. This sounds quite destructive, but once the flower spike appears the plant will die shortly thereafter anyway. A new plant will arise from underground portions of the old one. The central bud portion is what you want. Trim back all the leaves and wrap the "bud" in aluminum foil and place in a drip pan. Bake in a 350 degree oven for 10 hours. After cooking, peel off the leaves and scrape off the pulp much like you would eat an artichoke, working towards the center. If the heart is cooked long enough it should be a soft mushy golden brown.

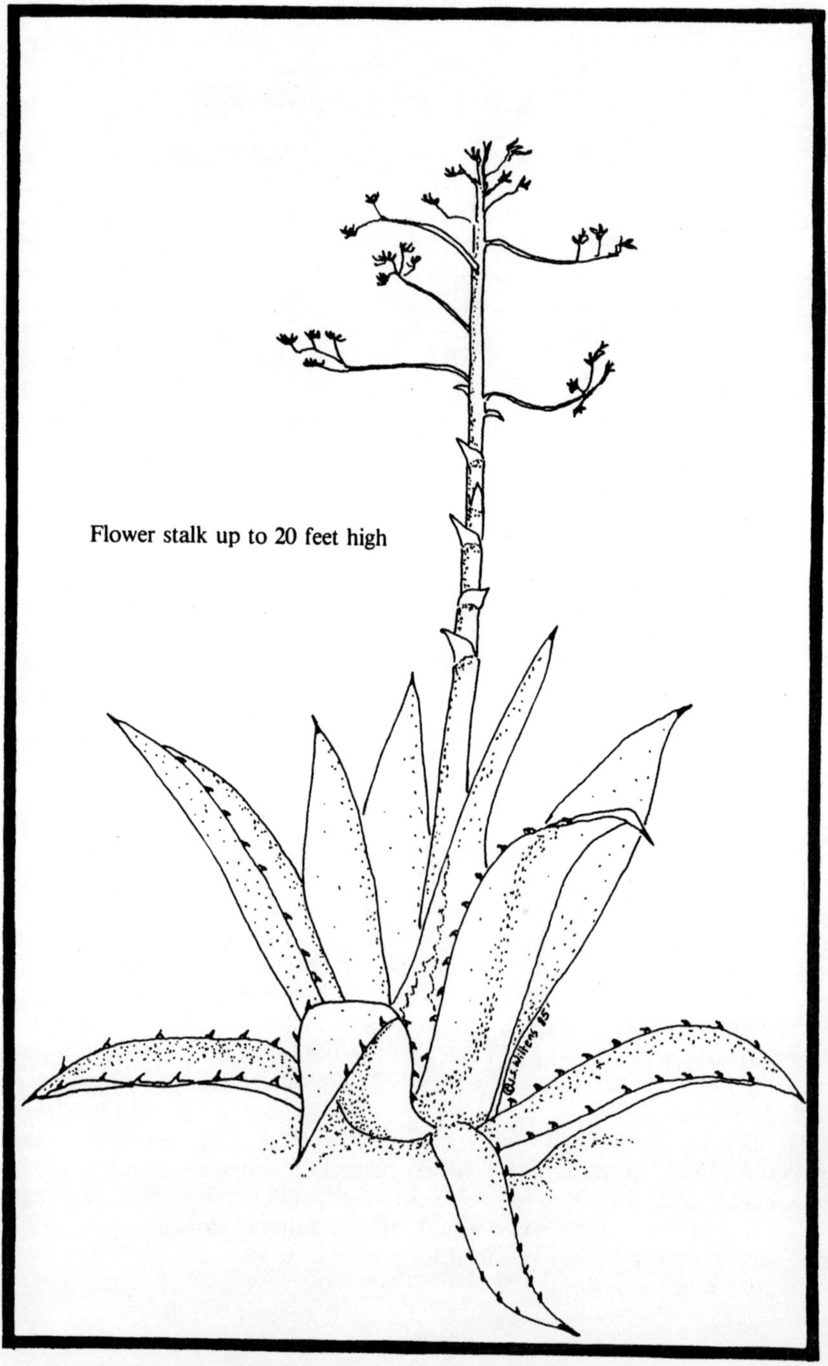

Agave (*Agave americana*)

INTERESTING FACTS: The Agave was a staple for many Indian tribes. The Mescalero Indians were so named by the Spanish due to their heavy use of the plant — the Spanish name for Agave is mescal. The Indians roasted the plants in large communal pits 10–12 feet in diameter and 3–4 feet deep. These pits can still be found in remote places in the Southwest.

A fine twine can be stripped from the leaves of the plant. If you carefully break off a spine, the attached fibers can be pulled from the plant and you have a ready made needle and thread. Some species of Agave have sharply curved spines on the leaf margin. I have twisted these off and with the threads that remain attached you have a fishing hook with a ready made leader. So fine is the cordage from Agave that in 1855 there was a plantation with 50 acres of *A. americana* planted at Key West, Florida for hemp production.

A large species of Mexican Agave is the source of tequila. The base of the plant is tapped for the sap which is fermented and then distilled.

The Aztecs would peel the surface layer off of Agave leaves and use them for paper. The early Spanish conquerors were so impressed with this that they used this paper to write their reports which were sent home to Spain. The Spanish archives still contain reports written on South America's answer to papyrus.

If you wish to make Agave paper, you will find it necessary to keep the pages sandwiched between something heavy so they will not curl up. Also, you must rub some glycerin into the parchment immediately after peeling it to keep it from becoming brittle.

AMARANTH

Amaranthus retroflexus
(Amaranth Family: Amaranthaceae)

OTHER NAMES: Pigweed, Redroot

DESCRIPTION: A stout, erect weed with alternate leaves. Long stalked leaves are widest near base with a blunt short pointed tip and a wavy margin. The tiny green flowers occur in dense spikes at the end of stems as well as in the axils of leaves. Rounded black seeds.

HABITAT: Common in vacant lots, waste areas and roadsides.

CAUTION: ***This plant has been shown to be capable of concentrating nitrates and has been implicated in livestock loss. Growing conditions were probably directly responsible for the toxic accumulation of nitrates. Excessive fertilizer and drought conditions can both cause problems.***

USES: As with many vegetables, Amaranth leaves are best picked at an early age, before the plant flowers. Prepare the greens as you would spinach. Due to its bland taste, the addition of curly dock and mustard leaves contributes a great deal to the taste.

Amaranth seeds were used by the Indians in making bread. Strip the seed heads into a paper bag. Spread the heads on a plastic sheet in the sun and allow to dry for several days. Use a broom handle and thrash the seed heads thoroughly to separate the seeds. Winnow by tossing the material into the air during a light breeze. Dry on a tray in the oven (375 degrees F.) for 30–40 minutes, stirring occasionally. Grind the seeds and use for a flour in making bread.

INTERESTING FACTS: Due to the persistent flowers of some species of Amaranth, the Greeks made this plant symbolic of immortality. The flowers were spread on graves to show their belief in the immortality of the soul.

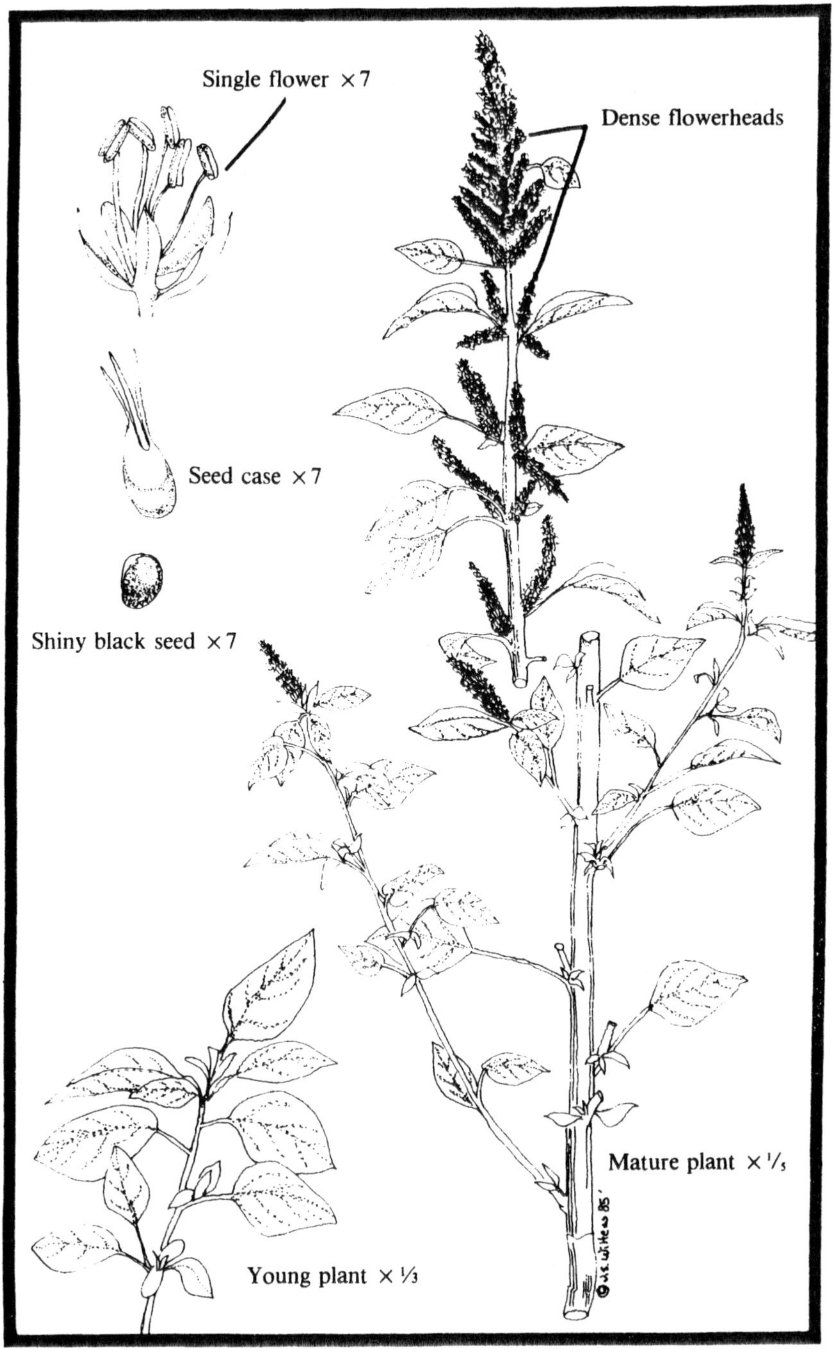

Amaranth (*Amaranthus retroflexus*)

BAY, CALIFORNIA

Umbellularia californica
(Laurel Family: Lauraceae)

OTHER NAMES: California Laurel, Mountain Laurel, Spice Bush

DESCRIPTION: Evergreen tree. Lance shaped leaves are arranged alternately on the branches. Leaves are a dark green on top and a light leathery green on the bottom, The leaves have a distinctive Bay spice odor. The tree can sometimes be found by smell alone. The flowers are in yellowish-white umbels. The round nut-like fruits have a green to purple fleshy covering. If the fleshy covering is removed, the nut shell is a light tan, the inner nut meat is greenish.

HABITAT: Common below 5000 feet. Hillsides, margins of streams and flatlands.

USES: Pick leaves and air dry. These leaves may be used in recipes calling for Bay. The commercial spice Bay comes from a different species of tree (*Lauris nobilis*). Because California Bay is more aromatic, about ⅓ less is needed in recipes calling for Bay.

Remove the dried nut meats from the shell and they may be eaten raw, though I find them quite bitter. Roasted nuts are more palatable. Spread whole dried nuts on a cookie sheet in a 350 degree oven for between 35 to 40 minutes. Taste test the roasting nuts occasionally so they are not scorched. Even with the roasting you will still find a somewhat bitter taste.

INTERESTING FACTS: A tea brewed from the leaves was used as a disinfectant by early settlers.

Bay leaves act as a natural insect repellent. California Indians used to fumigate their lodges by burning a bough of Bay. A dog collar of woven leaves helps to repel fleas. Packets of leaves placed in cupboards seem to deter a variety of insects.

In Oregon, where the trees grow quite large, the Bay tree is called Myrtle and provides a wood prized for its fine grain.

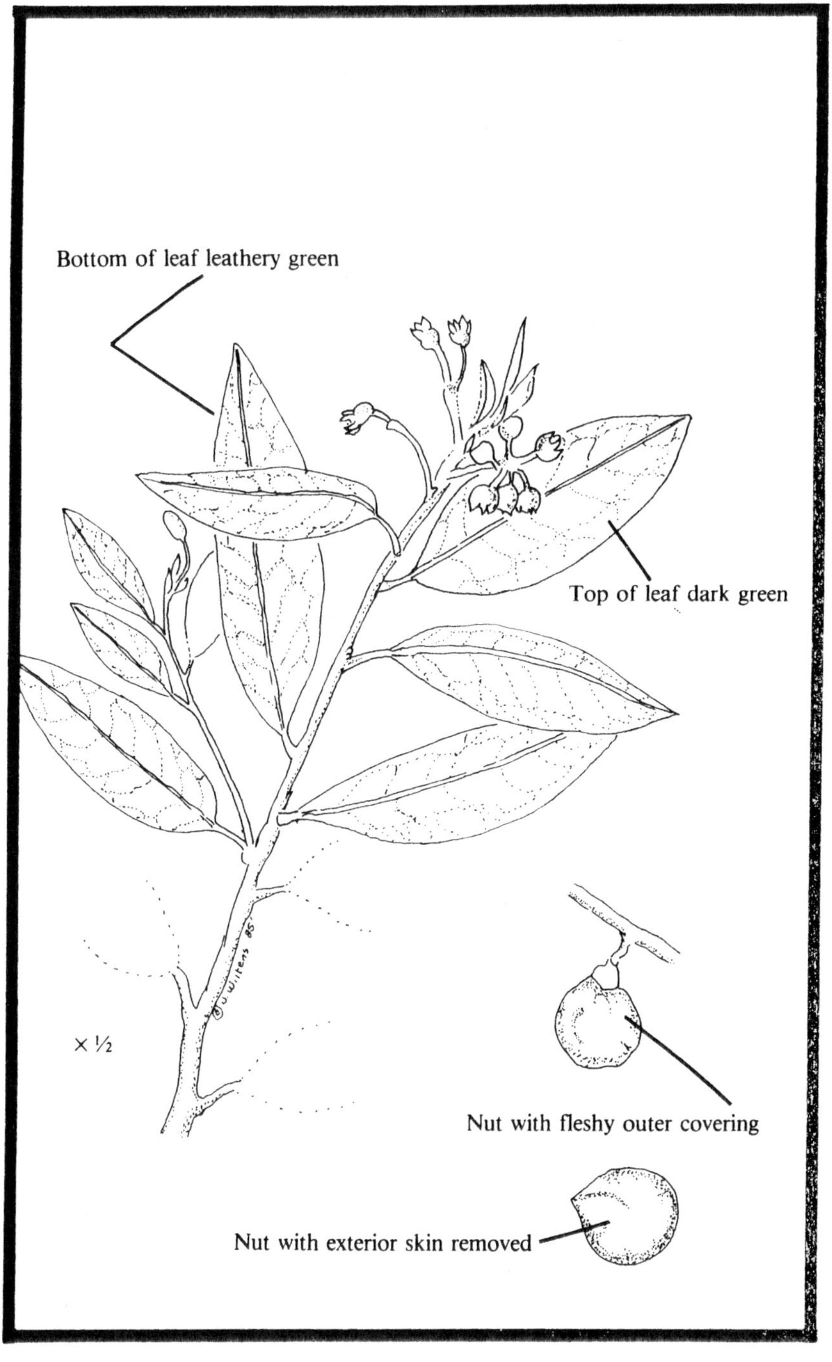

Bay, California (*Umbellularia californica*)

BLACKBERRY

Rubus ursinus
(Rose Family: Rosaceae)

OTHER NAMES: California Blackberry, Bramble Bush, Dewberry

DESCRIPTION: Tough trailing vines with wicked thorns give Blackberry the synonym — plant barbwire. Leaflets have a rough serrated edge and are grouped in threes. The white flowers have 5 petals. The berry is a compact cluster of shiny black globes which do not pull away from the central core. The *Rubus* genus contains a number of species which can be used in a manner similar to *R. ursinus.*

HABITAT: Disturbed sites, along trails and roads, canyons, open woodlands, abandoned farmland.

CAUTION: *Avoid the obvious thorns.*

One oblique problem with Blackberries is that some people get them confused with another more sinister plant. I'll never forget taking my younger brother for a nature walk with my parents' admonishment to keep him away from any poison oak. They thought that if he was even in the proximity of the plant he would develop a rash. This was based on a number of unfortunate attacks of poison oak, even though he was absolutely positive he had never contacted the plant. During our walk he cautioned me on brushing up against some poison oak. I turned and all I could see were Blackberry vines. He patiently told me that you had to beware of plants with "leaves of three" and "stickers." For years he had been under the misconception that Blackberry was poison oak. Of course poison oak does not have "stickers," the thorns are found only on Blackberries. The three-leaf-pattern that is shared by both poison oak and some species of Blackberries makes it imperative that you make sure your plant has "stickers" before touching the foliage. Do not take a chance on a case of mistaken identity.

USES: Blackberries taste great fresh. Some of the best berries I've had were obtained while floating in a raft down the Klamath River. The plants grow in dense thickets along the waters' edge and only rafters, trout (Yes, fish will eat berries that fall in the water) and the occasional bird are in competition for the fully ripened fruit.

Jams and jellies can be made from the fruit. Just refer to the directions in a box of pectin.

A very simple jam can be made with the following recipe:

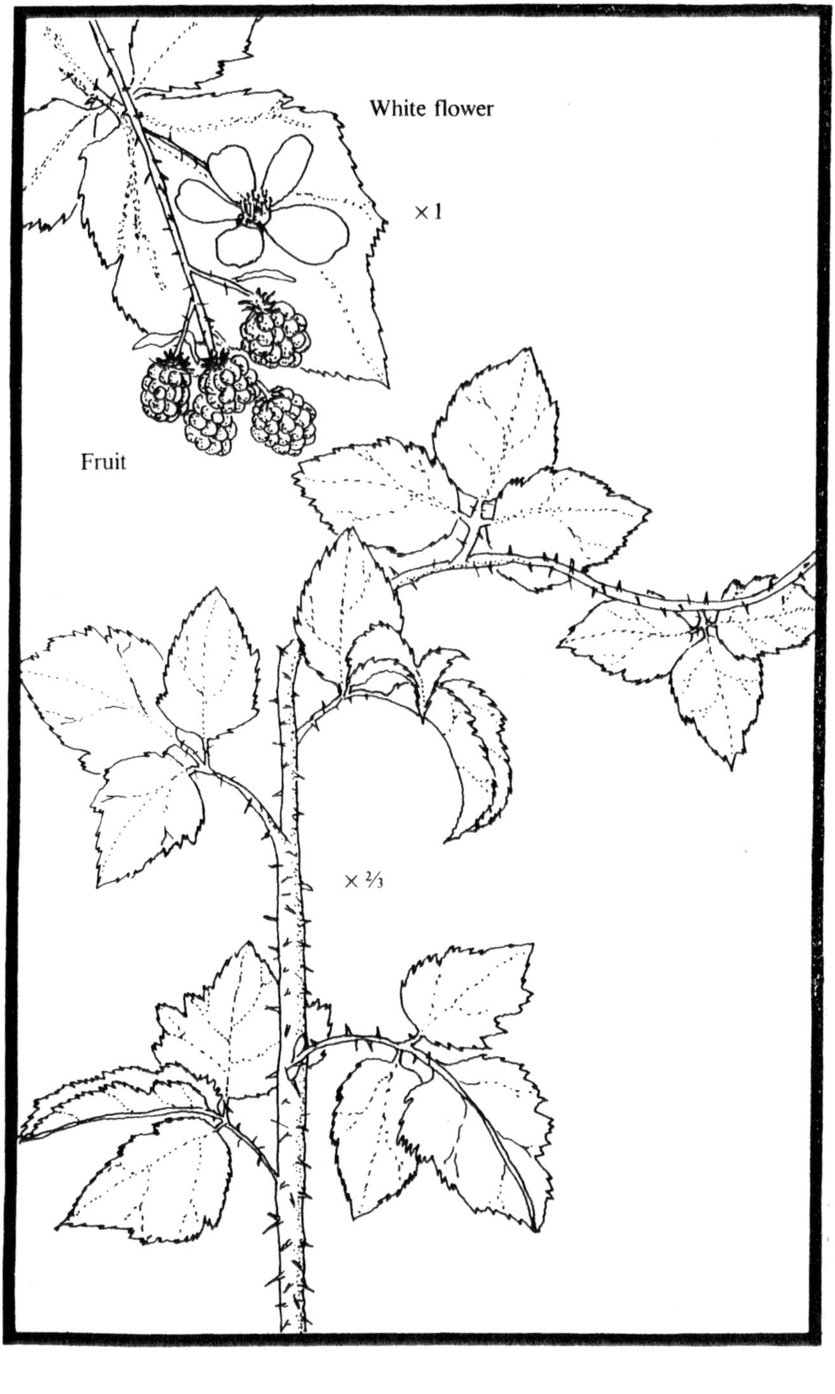

Blackberry (*Rubus ursinus*)

CIVIL WAR JAM

4 cups Blackberries
2 cups brown sugar

Stir the sugar and Blackberries together and mash. Boil the mixture gently over low heat for thirty minutes to an hour. The resultant jam may be stored in your freezer or can be poured hot and sealed in sterile jars.

INTERESTING FACTS: This particular species of Blackberry was the plant from which the Boysenberry, Youngberry and Loganberry were derived.

During the Civil War, the blue and grey troops would often make a truce so that the men could go foraging for Blackberries. The berries were thought to be helpful in preventing dysentery and certain stomach disorders. It must have been felt that the men's health was more important than the war — at least at the moment.

BRACKEN FERN

Pteridium aquilinum
(Fern Family: Pteridaceae)

OTHER NAMES: Brake, Wa-ra-be (Japanese)

DESCRIPTION: Just after emerging from the ground, Bracken has a characteristic fiddlehead shape, a tightly curled leaf cluster borne on a stalk. As the plant matures the fiddlehead uncurls. The leaf divisions become progressively more simple as you proceed from the base of the stalk to the top. At the base of the stalk what appears as an array of leaves is actually a compound leaf. The plant may be covered with a rusty colored felt.

HABITAT: Moist places, forest floor.

CAUTION: Bracken has long been used as a food. It was eaten extensively by the Indians, is still a preferred food in Japan and can be found on the menus of a number of fancy restaurants in the New England States. ***But there may be some risk. The evidence is more suggestive than conclusive. In most cases it is the older leaves that have been implicated in poisoning when fed to livestock over a prolonged period. It is known that Bracken contains thiaminase, an enzyme responsible for the breakdown of thiamine, which can result in vitamin B_1 deficiency if uncooked Bracken is consumed in large quantities. There is also a small unidentified molecule that destroys cells in the bone marrow of cattle resulting in a loss of white blood cells and impaired clotting of red blood cells. It must be mentioned that a cow fed exclusively on a diet of mature Bracken leaves for two months does not necessarily approximate the human equivalent of an occasional side dish of cooked Bracken fiddleheads. I should also mention that laboratory rats fed Bracken as the predominant part of their diet have developed stomach cancer.***

What this means to the forager is to definitely avoid consumption of the older fronds. And for whatever it is worth, I have eaten the young fiddleheads after cooking and found them to be delicious, but I restrict my intake to a reasonable quantity on special occasions. You'll have to make your own decision.

USES: The fiddleheads are collected while still tightly curled. A light reddish fuzz adheres to the outside of the curled leaves. Some books tell you to remove this fuzz. This is easier said than done. In general I just wash the fiddleheads under water as you would normally do for any vegetable and it is sufficient. Steam the fiddleheads for 5 minutes and serve with butter.

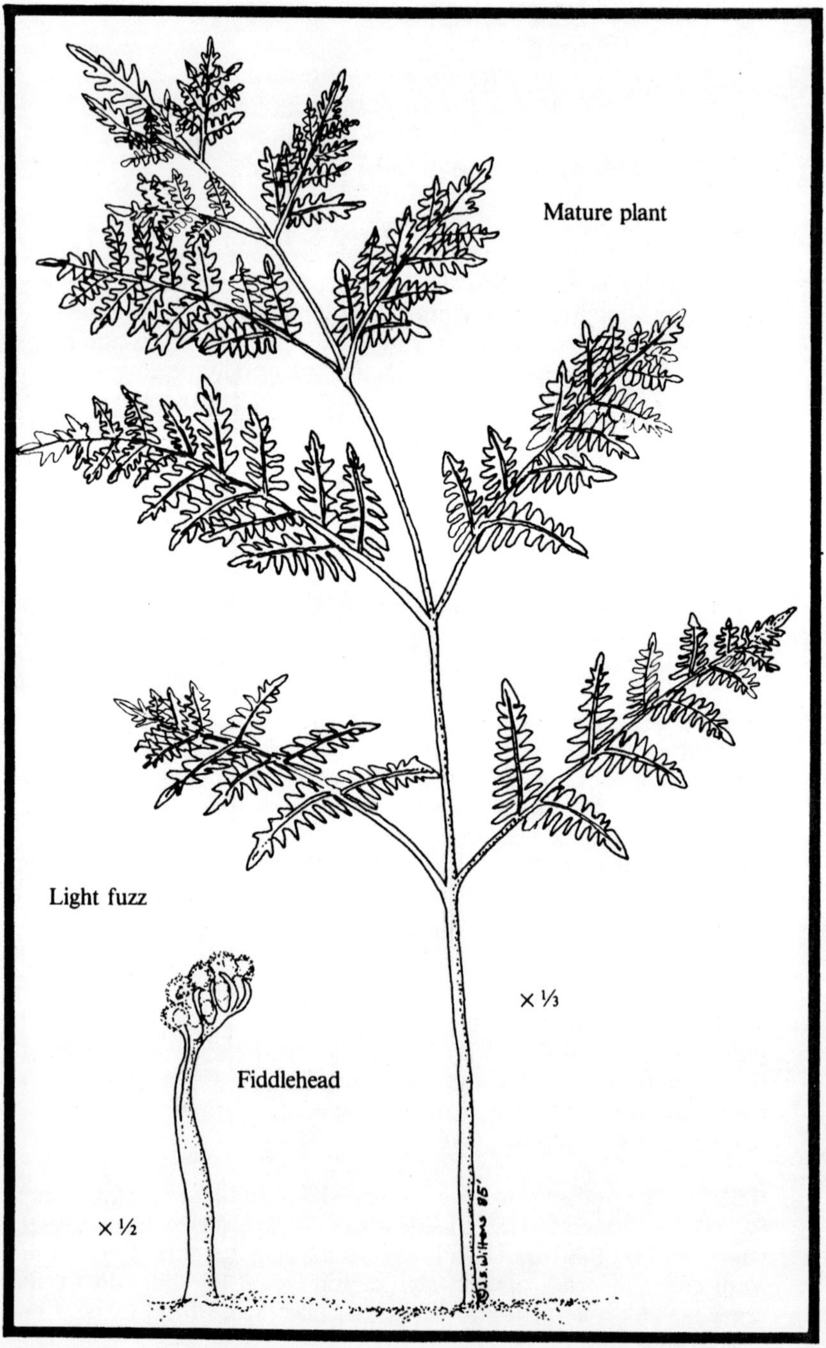

Bracken Fern (*Pteridium aquilinum*)

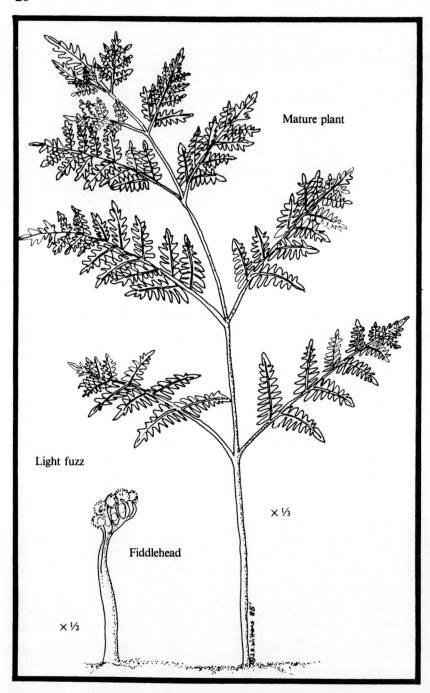

INTERESTING FACTS: I have found older dried Bracken leaves to make excellent bedding. Deer also seem fond of finding a dense stand of Bracken and using it for their boudoir. Not only will deer sleep on the old fronds but they will compete with you for the young fiddleheads. A good deer area can often be found by looking for tall Bracken stalks with nothing but a dried tip. The deer have nipped off the young fiddlehead, the plant is condemned to remain leafless but the stalk continues to elongate.

During times of famine, people have used the tough rhizome of Bracken to make a flour. It is reputed that in 1745 the duke of Orleans gave Louis XV a piece of bread made of fern and said, "Sire, this is what your subjects live upon." I doubt this "sharing of bread" endeared the duke to the king.

CATTAIL

Typha latifolia
(Cat-tail Family: Typhaceae)

OTHER NAMES: Soft Flag, Cossack Asparagus, Bulrush

DESCRIPTION: A rhizome producing erect sword-shaped leaf blades with parallel venation. The flower spikes resemble a felt-upholstered hot dog on a skewer.

CAUTION: ***Cattails are commonly found growing in marshy water, which in our locale often has the possibility of being polluted. I am careful to choose plants from areas I believe to be relatively clean. To assure biological purity, any portions of the plant that I use are sterilized.***

The sterilization can be part of the processing procedure, such as when you use Cattail flour which is baked in a hot oven, or if I want to use a part raw, such as the young shoots, then I soak them in water containing purification tablets of the sort used to disinfect water (Aqua-Pure is a brand name for an iodide disinfectant).

USES: Almost all parts of the Cattail are useful. The green bloom spikes (the portion that will later turn into the characteristic brown heads) can be steamed for 10–20 minutes, smothered in butter and eaten like corn on the cob.

When the yellow pollen is evident on the spikes, it can be collected by placing a bag around the heads and shaking vigorously. This pollen can be mixed with an equal volume of whole wheat flour to make pancakes, muffins and bread.

One of the biggest food sources available from the Cattail is contained in the underground portion, the rhizomes. Wade into the water, reach down along the stem to the rhizome. Get your hand as far along the rhizome as you can and pull up. You will need about a shopping bag worth of rhizomes which will be used to make Cattail flour.

To prepare the rhizomes, rinse in water and pull off the fibrous roots. With a sharp knife, trim off the outer spongy layer, working back to the leaf base. If you cut the rhizome sideways you will note a cental core with a slippery texture. This core is the starch you are working to retrieve. Put about a quarter cup of water in a blender, slowly add the peeled cores, not so fast that they jam the blender blade. Pour the resultant slurry through a metal mesh strainer. The strainer will remove the fibers from the starch. It will be necessary to mash the slurry in the strainer to retrieve as much starch as possible. Discard the fibers. Add

Cattail (*Typha latifolia*)

about 4 volumes of water to the starch and stir. Let the starch settle overnight, decant the water off from the starch. The starch may be dried for storage or used as is.

SWAMP BISCUITS

1 cup dried Cattail flour
2 tsps baking powder
4 pinches salt
8 tsps solid shortening
½ cup milk

Preheat oven to 450 degrees. In a bowl, sift together flour, baking powder and salt. Use 2 knives to cut shortening into flour mixture until crumbly. Make a well in center, pour in milk all at once and stir with a fork until dough cleans sides of bowl. Drop by teaspoons onto a greased baking sheet. Makes 12 biscuits.

The young buds may be snapped from the rhizomes and eaten raw (refer to preceding caution) or stir fried in an oriental fashion.

INTERESTING FACTS: In the 1940's there was an interest in establishing commercial Cattail farms. Research showed that a single acre of Cattails could produce 32 tons of processed flour. This exceeds the productive capacity for many domesticated grain crops. But there was just never sufficient interest and this crop is still the domain of the wild food enthusiast.

The leaves have been used for many years in rustic furniture as webbing. To prepare Cattail leaves for weaving, collect the longest leaves you can find, tie them in bundles for drying (this prevents them from shrinking later on) and suspend from the rafters in your garage for several months. To weave the leaves, soak them in water to make them pliable.

Many of the old orange yoke life vests were filled with kapok, the downy fuzz from the Cattail spike. Kapok has been pretty much replaced with synthetic air-celled foams. Kapok was also a filler in cheap sleeping bags many years ago.

CHICKWEED

Stellaria media
(Pink Family: Caryophyllaceae)

OTHER NAMES: Starwort

DESCRIPTION: The weak succulent stem is either prostrate or supported by other plants. A line of tiny hairs runs the length of the stem. Leaves are oval and opposite. Flowers arise from side branches in the leaf axils. At first glance the white flowers appear to have ten petals, on closer inspection each petal can be seen to be split part way down. The green sepals are longer than the petals.

HABITAT: Prefers moist and wet areas. Often in disturbed sites, open woodlands and shaded areas.

USES: This plant can be used raw in salad or boiled and served like spinach. The young growing tips are best, as the older portions tend to be stringy.

INTERESTING FACTS: Chickweed tends to be high in copper and vitamin C.

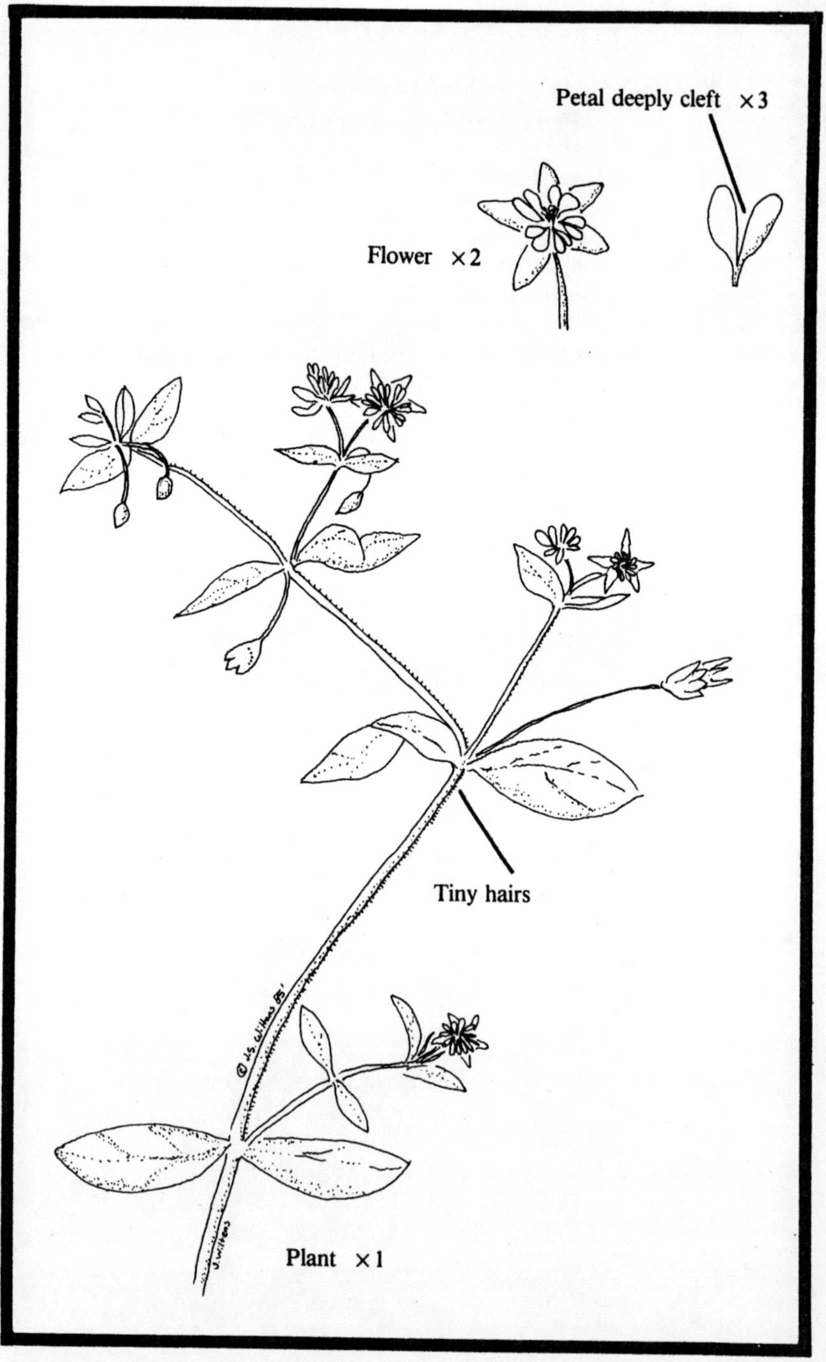

Chickweed (*Stellaria media*)

CHICORY

Cichorium intybus
(Sunflower Family: Compositae)

OTHER NAMES: Succory, Barbe de Capuchin (French), Blue Sailors

DESCRIPTION: Rosette of leaves arises from a deep taproot. Dandelion shaped leaves have a deeply toothed and ragged appearance, often with a red mid-vein. The erect flower stem bears sky-blue flowers spaced up its length. The flower petals have a tattered appearance due to 5 notches at the end of each petal. Stems produce a milky sap when broken (a characteristic of many members of the Sunflower family).

HABITAT: Disturbed areas, roadsides, fields, vacant lots.

USES: Chicory is cultivated in a number of European countries and sold as a vegetable. It can be used fresh in salads, steamed as a potherb or the root used as a coffee substitute.

It is important to pick young Chicory leaves, well before flowering, as the leaves become very bitter with age. Chop the young leaves and add to salads. If the leaves are beginning to turn bitter, boil in one or two changes of water, and serve as a potherb.

Chicory has long been used as a coffee substitute, with none of the caffeine. Dig up the roots and scrub briskly under running water. Slice the root thinly and dry in the sun. Roast the dried root in the oven until it turns a light brown, then grind. Not being a coffee fan myself, I find the finished product somewhat bitter but people who like strong coffee apparently appreciate the taste.

INTERESTING FACTS: In France, Chicory has an elitist position among vegetable delicacies. Boards are placed over the young plants, without light the leaves do not develop chlorophyll (the substance that gives the green color to leaves). The blanched leaves are served under the alias, *Barbe de capuchin*, in the finest restaurants.

Chicory is commercially grown in a number of European countries. Growers attempted to start farms in the U.S. in the early 20th century, but interest was not sufficiently strong, and producers have been sporadic. I've noticed that a number of Bay Area markets will occasionally offer Chicory in their produce sections.

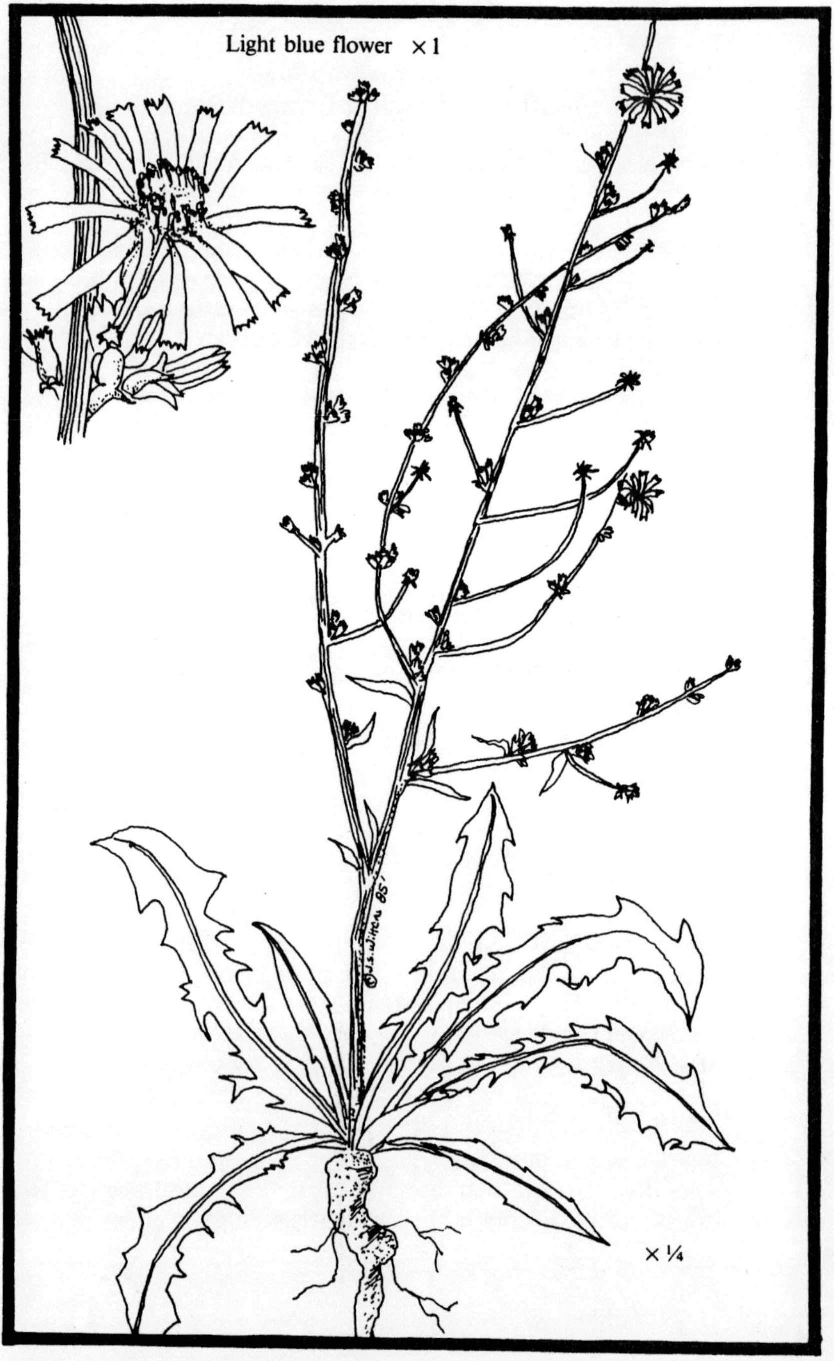

Chicory (*Cichorium intybus*)

DANDELION

Taraxacum officinale
(Compositae: Sunflower Family)

OTHER NAMES: Blowball, Common Dandelion

DESCRIPTION: A perennial, composed of a basal rosette of leaves arising from a taproot. Leaves are oblong to spatulate with deep indentations giving the appearance of teeth on an old rip saw. When plants are found growing in tall grass or shade, the leaves are often upright. In another environment, such as a frequently mown lawn, the leaves may be prostrate. Flower buds start near the center of the leaf rosette. As the season progresses, the bright yellow flowers appear. Each flower head is composed of numerous individual flowers crowded together. The flower heads are borne on the end of a hollow stalk which rises from an inch to a foot above the ground. As the flower head matures it develops into the cottony ball, containing seeds, that children are so fond of blowing into the wind. The leaves and stalks exude a milky juice when cut.

HABITAT: Lawns, waste places, fields, roadsides.

USES: Virtually every part of the Dandelion is edible. The leaves, roots, flowers and seed heads are all potential food sources.

Leaves can be collected in early spring before the flower or tufted seed heads appear. Use the leaves fresh in a salad with a little oil and vinegar or as a garnish for a sandwich. As the leaves age they become increasingly bitter and may require steaming or boiling in several changes of water to remove the bitter taste. You can familiarize yourself with the palatability stages by finding a stand of Dandelions and taste-testing the plant during the course of a season.

The roots serve a dual use. They can be prepared in a manner similar to parsnips or used as a coffee substitute. Dig up the spring roots and thoroughly wash them. Then boil them in two changes of water, with a pinch of baking soda added to the first water. Serve seasoned with salt, pepper and butter.

For a non-caffeine coffee substitute, clean, dry to brittleness and grind. Brew like coffee. Tastes a great deal like commercial Postum.

The flower buds may be boiled for 3–5 minutes then served with butter. When the buds have flowered, take the flower heads and swirl them in a pancake batter and fry.

The flowers have another use in the well known Dandelion wine.

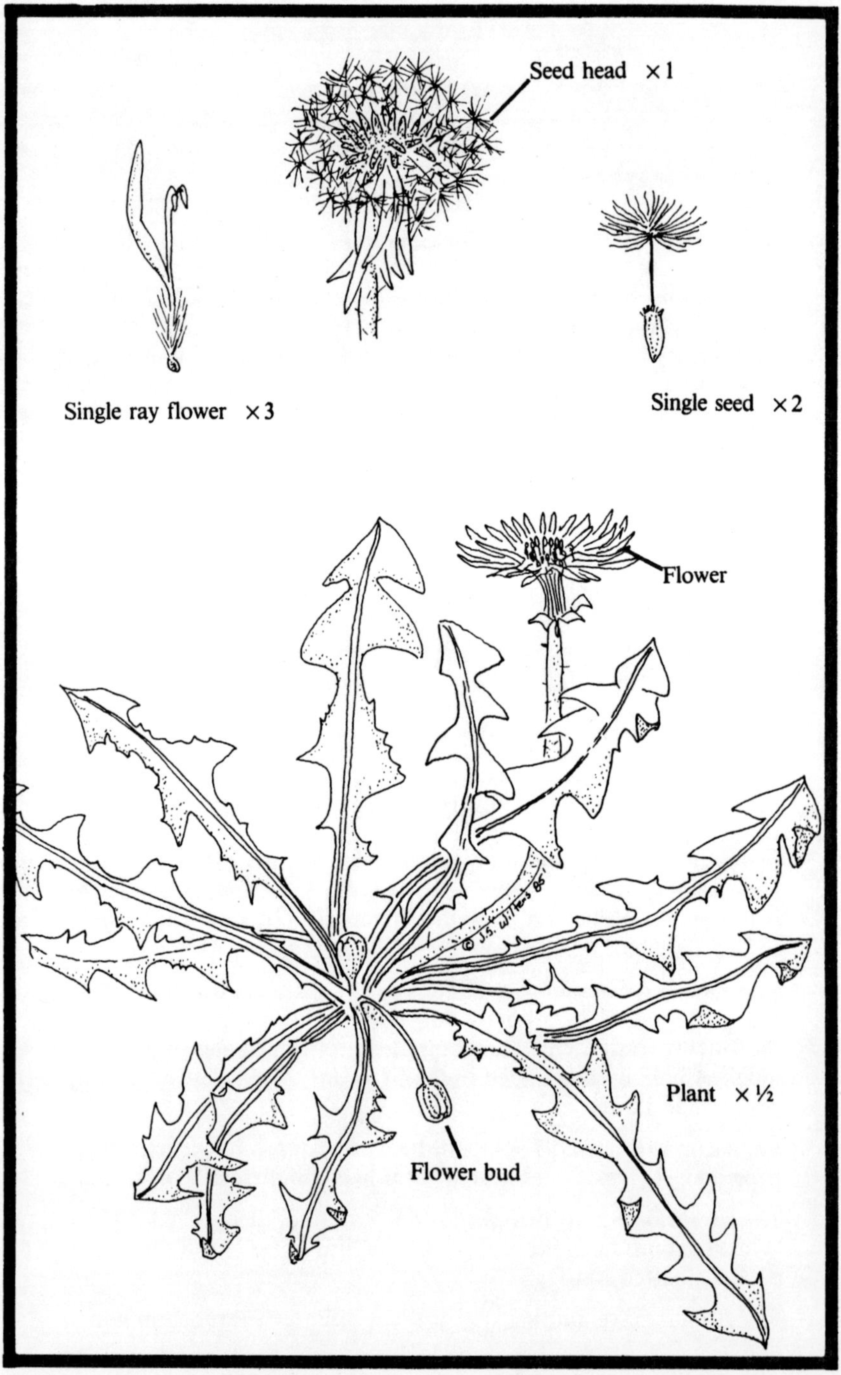

Dandelion (*Taraxacum officinale*)

Finally we come to the little parachute seeds. In an emergency, even this part of the Dandelion provides a food source. Pull the tufted seeds from their stalk and rub them vigorously between your palms. The seeds, shorn of their little parachutes, will drop through your palms to a clean surface. With a little careful winnowing the rest of the downy fuzz can be removed from the seeds. Though somewhat bitter, the seeds could be an important survival food addition.

INTERESTING FACTS: Dandelion has a healthy reputation. In a comparison of fresh Dandelion greens with lettuce, Dandelion had approximately three times as much protein, twelve times as much vitamin A and three times as much vitamin C. It also ranked higher in a number of other minerals and vitamins.

The white milky sap that exudes from the broken stems and leaves of Dandelions is a natural rubber. During WW II a Russian species of Dandelion, *T. kok-saghyz*, was cultivated in Poland as an alternative rubber source. This plant has a rubber content as high as twenty percent, whereas the common Dandelion is closer to one percent.

The common name, Dandelion, is derived from *dent de lion* (teeth of the lion), referring to the shape of the leaves.

DOCK

Rumex crispus
(Buckwheat Family: Polygonaceae)

OTHER NAMES: Curly Dock, Spurdock

DESCRIPTION: A perennial. The upright lance-shaped leaves have a distinct wavy pattern along the leaf margin and an obvious leaf midrib. The leaf petioles have a groove that runs from the leaf to the stem. Young leaves are rolled into a pencil shape, uncurling with maturity. As the plant ages it sends out an upright stalk from 1 to 4 feet in height. The hollow stems turn from green to red as they mature. Numerous inconspicuous green flowers arise on side branches from the leaf axils. The tiny seeds are borne on a dry membranous three winged structure.

HABITAT: Common in disturbed sites, fields, roadsides and vacant lots.

CAUTIONS: ***The pleasant sour taste of Dock is due to the presence of oxalates. Oxalates are a good reason to consume this plant in reasonable quantities as there are reported cases of poisoning in livestock after consuming large quantities of R. acetosa, a related species.***

USES: Dock leaves make an excellent spinach substitute. Pick the youngest leaves before the floral stalk forms. When you pull these young leaves from the plant you will notice that they are covered with a thin membranous sheet. Steamed for three to five minutes, these leaves have a taste similar to spinach with lemon added to it.

Fresh leaves may also be chopped and used raw in a salad. Due to their tart flavor, Dock should be mixed with bland greens.

Older leaves can be used but will require longer boiling and for really old leaves it may be necessary to use several changes of water.

Dock leaves have a taste reminiscent of rhubarb and can be used to make a very interesting pie:

MOCK RHUBARB PIE

4½ cups firmly packed Dock leaves and stems
⅛ cup flour
1 tbsp cornstarch
1 tbsp butter
½ tsp cinnamon
1 dash of lemon juice
2 crust pie shell (unbaked 9")

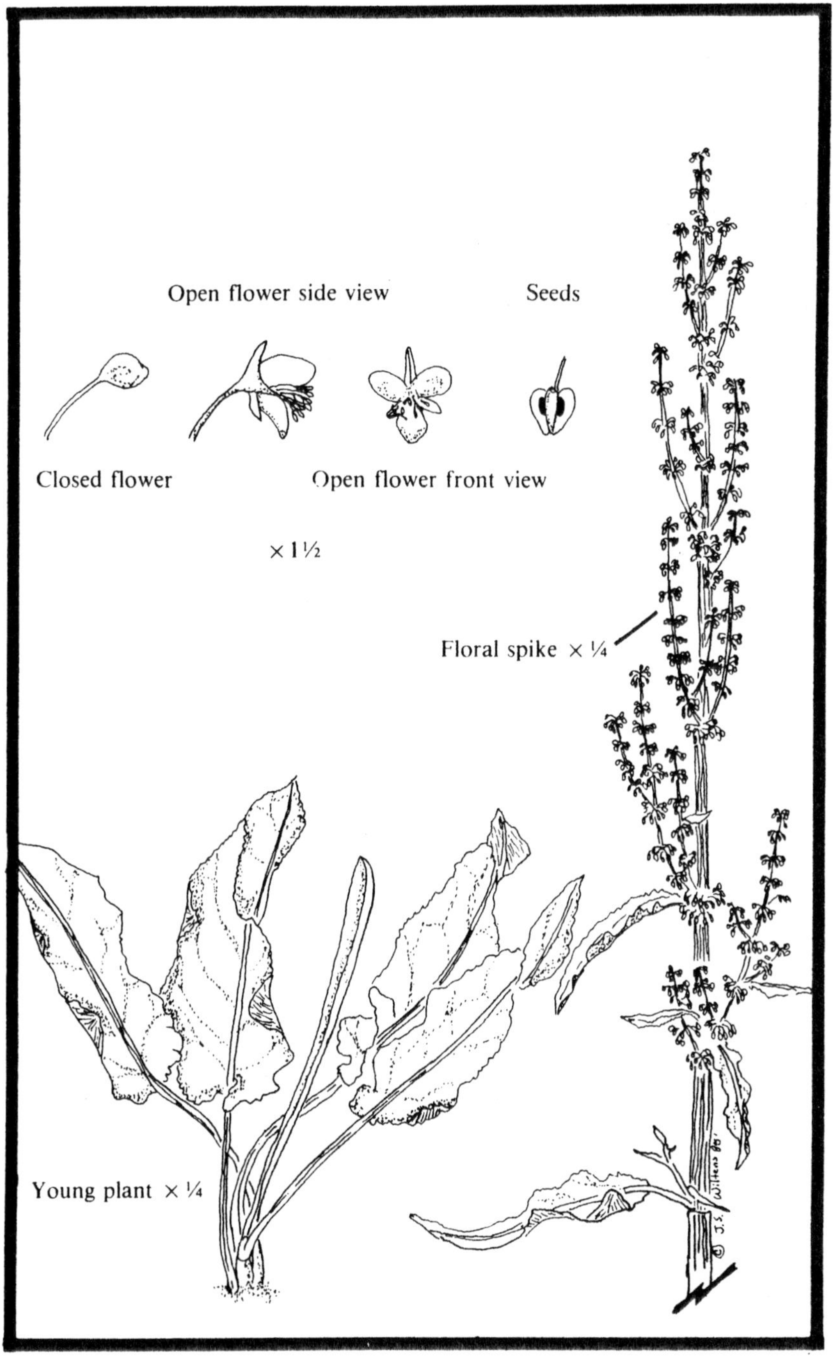

Dock (*Rumex crispus*)

Chop Dock leaves into 1'' pieces and add sufficient water to just cover. Steam or boil until leaves wilt (you should have about 2½ cups of cooked Dock). Drain and add flour, cornstarch, butter, cinnamon and lemon juice. Mix thoroughly. Preheat oven to 375 degrees. Pour into pie shell, cover with top crust and bake for 50 minutes.

In a survival situation, the tiny seeds can be threshed and winnowed from the dry brown seed stalks. The amount of work required, and the low yield, relegate the seeds to emergency fare. The Indians would grind the seeds and use them as a flour substitute or mash and soak them in water to make a life-sustaining gruel.

INTERESTING FACTS: The genus name *Rumex* is derived from the Roman ''to suck.'' The tart leaves were sucked by Roman soldiers to help allay thirst on long marches.

The characteristic sour flavor of Dock is found in another member of the Buckwheat family, rhubarb. The well known tart taste of rhubarb pie comes from using the petioles of this plant. While it is common knowledge that the petioles are edible it is not as well known that the leaf blade is toxic. The leaves contain high levels of oxalic acid. Oxalic acid combines with calcium in the body to form crystals that can damage the kidneys severely. Deaths have been reported from eating rhubarb leaves. A rash of poisonings occurred in England during WW I. An unknowledgeable government official, in an effort to conserve food, made the recommendation that rhubarb leaves be eaten and not thrown away. Even though the error was discovered and a prompt retraction issued, there were many serious poisonings and a number of deaths.

Dock leaves are higher in vitamin C than oranges and higher in vitamin A than carrots.

Indians used the dried leaves as a non-nicotine tobacco substitute.

ELDERBERRY

Sambucus mexicana
(Honeysuckle Family: Caprifoliaceae)

DESCRIPTION: Shrubs or trees. There are an odd number of leaflets on each leaf stem, usually 3 or 5. Leaf margin is finely serrated. If you break off a twig you will notice a large central pith with a soft consistency. The small flowers are clustered in dense umbels. The fruit is a round BB-sized blue berry dusted with a whitish bloom in dense hanging clumps.

HABITAT: Roadsides, rich soil, woodland margins, cut over areas.

CAUTION: ***Some caution needs to be exercised in using Elderberry. Though the cooked berries are commonly used in pies and jellies, the leaves, bark, young buds, and in some cases the berry itself, have been implicated in poisoning. Species with red or white berries should be avoided.***

There are cases of children hollowing out the soft pith in Elderberry branches to make pea-shooters and flutes and subsequently being poisoned.

There is a recipe for Elderberry flowers that is found in a large number of edible plant books. It consists of gathering the umbels of flowers just as the blossoms open and dipping them in a fritter batter and deep fat frying them. I and several friends have tried this on several occasions and, though it hasn't exactly made us sick, I find it to rank as one of the fastest acting laxatives known to man. My friends are quick (yes, very quick) to agree with me. For this reason I am somewhat hesitant to give a positive recommendation on using the flowers (*S. mexicana*), even though a number of other authors mention no such laxative problem. Indians of the Pacific Northwest were known to use another species of Elderberry (*S. glauca*) for purgative purposes, though they relied on a decoction of the bark.

USES: The taste of fresh berries is somewhat variable depending on the locale of harvesting. On the other hand, jams and jellies made from cooked berries are excellent.

ELDERBERRY JAM

3 lbs. Elderberries destemmed
juice from one lemon
1 box Sure-Jell (commercial pectin)
4 cups sugar

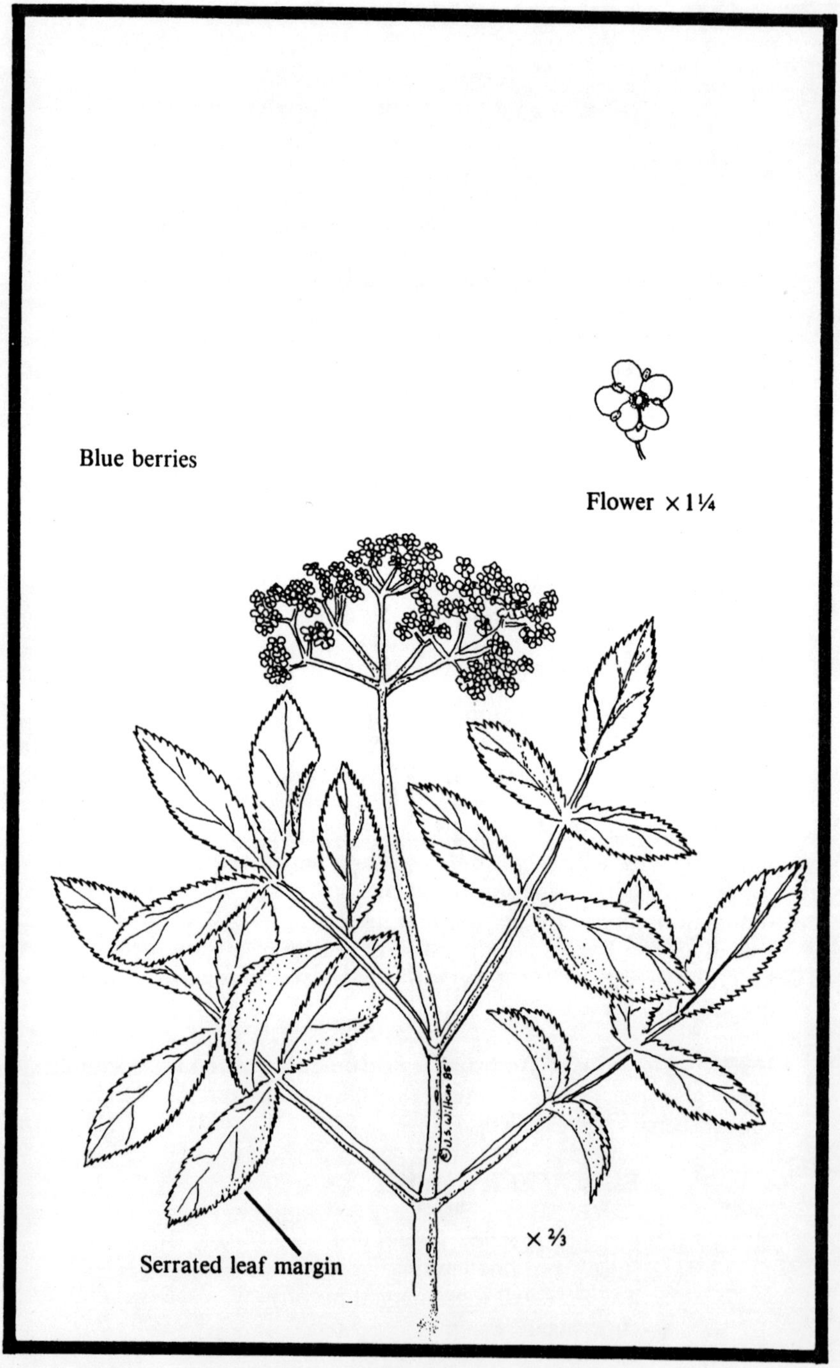

Elderberry (*Sambucus mexicana*)

Mash Elderberries and simmer for 15 minutes. Add lemon juice and *Sure-Jell*, mix and bring to a boil for 1 minute, stirring constantly. Dump in sugar and bring to a hard boil for 2 minutes, stirring constantly. Remove from heat and pour into sterilized Mason jars and cap with sterilized caps.

Elderberry wine can also be made from the berries.

INTERESTING FACTS: Elderberry is one of nature's richest sources of vitamin C.

The stems have been used to make arrow shafts, whistles and flutes, the latter two uses sometimes causing illness.

Sambucus is derived from the Greek "Sambuke," a musical instrument made from Elder wood.

Some historians have suggested that the Cross of Christ was made from the wood of Elder.

EUCALYPTUS

Eucalyptus sps.
(Myrtle Family: Myrtaceae)

OTHER NAMES: Gum Tree

DESCRIPTION: Tall trees with persistent or shredding bark. Scythe shaped leaves are a dull grey-green and hang with their tips pointing down. Flowers are composed of a warty cap, the numerous stamens arising from the cap give it a delicate appearance. When the stamens fall off, the warty cap has an X-shaped keyhole in the center.

HABITAT: Coast, coastal hills, valleys and deserts.

USES: A strong tea can be brewed from the leaves which helps in opening clogged sinuses. The woody fruits can be sucked for a sore throat though the taste is somewhat overpowering.

INTERESTING FACTS: Eucalyptus is a recent import to the United States. The first seeds were brought to California in 1856. Because the plant has been imported solely by seed, no natural pests have come to the Americas with this plant. In Australia you seldom find a Eucalyptus leaf that hasn't been chewed by some insect, while in California you will rarely find one that has been chewed.

I can remember spending weeks in a Eucalyptus grove during the summer. While insects were prevalent in the surrounding area, the grove itself was relatively insect free. This is due to the repellent quality of these mildly aromatic trees. Dog and cat bedding filled with Eucalyptus leaves acts as a safe repellent for fleas.

Some species of Eucalyptus put on 10–15 feet of growth a year in the initial years.

The drooping leaf of the Eucalyptus is an adaptation thought to compensate for the intense light and heat the plant would experience in its native habitat, Australia. Chlorophyll is decomposed by strong light and heat. By hanging vertically with only their thin edges directed towards the light, the leaves of Eucalyptus are better suited to a harsh climate.

When Eucalyptus leaves are ground and the oils removed by distillation, the substance cinerole is obtained, an efficient bactericide.

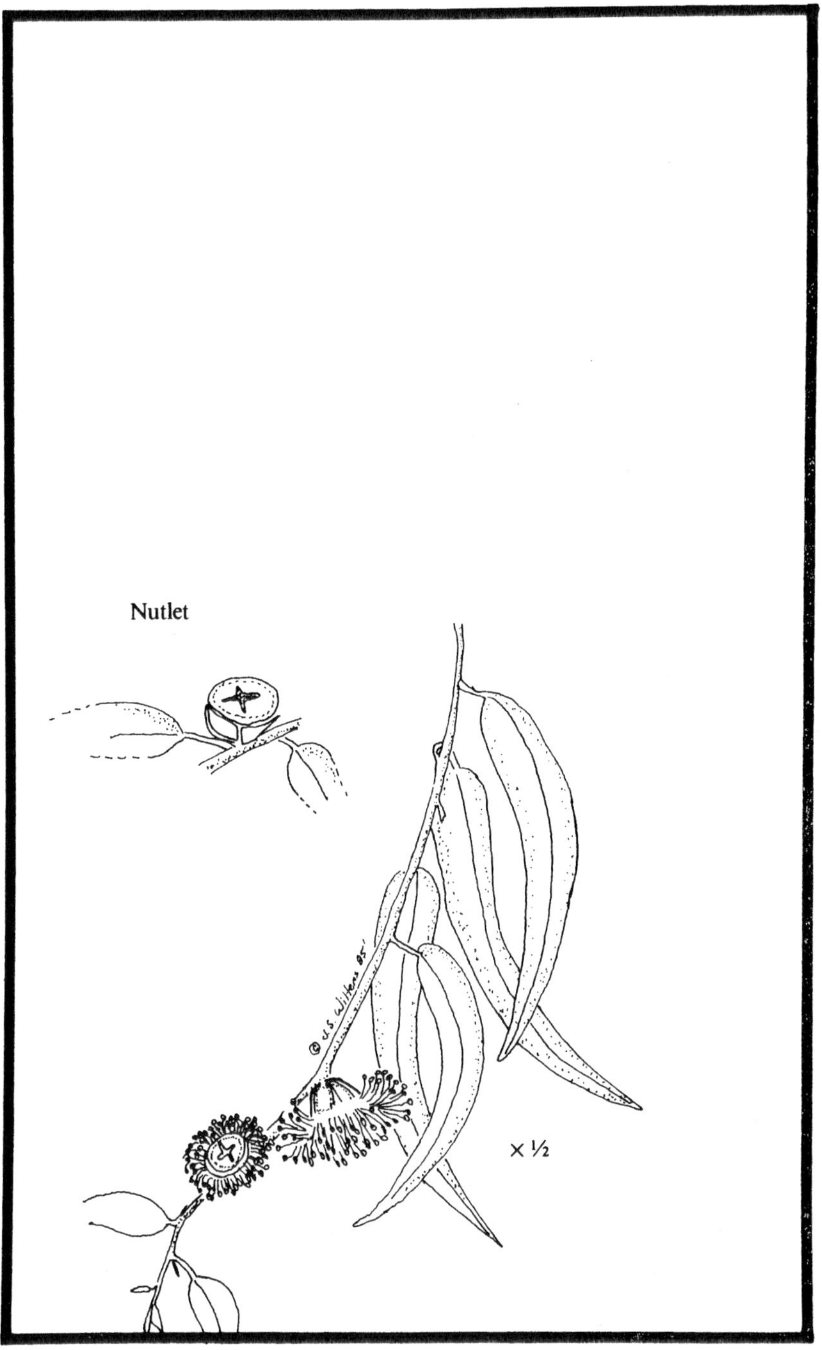

Eucalyptus (*Eucalyptus sp.*)

FENNEL

Foeniculum vulgare
(Carrot Family: Umbelliferae)

OTHER NAMES: Anise, Wild Licorice

DESCRIPTION: The clumped leaf stalks look almost fern-like at a distance. On closer inspection, the leaves can be seen to be finely divided and thread-like. Plants have a blue-green cast due to a thin waxy covering. The leaf stalk is comparable to celery. The yellow flowers are arranged in large compound umbels. As the season progresses the hollow flowering stalks become woody and bear the ribbed seeds. All parts of the plant have a licorice odor.

HABITAT: Common in waste places, roadsides, vacant lots, fence rows.

CAUTION: ***Some people have confused Fennel with another member of the carrot family, poison hemlock (Conium maculatum). Learn to recognize the differences between these two plants and remember that Fennel has a characteristic licorice odor.***

USES: The tender stalks of newly emergent Fennel can be eaten raw like celery. If you have ever nibbled on the finely branched thread-like leaves you will notice a strong licorice taste. The celery shaped stalks have a considerably milder taste than the leaves.

The green stalks may also be boiled and used in a variety of dishes. Boiling or steaming removes much of the licorice taste. Two of my favorite recipes:

FENNEL IN ORANGE-BUTTER SAUCE

2 cups Fennel stems
⅛ cube butter
2 tbsps orange juice

Cut Fennel into ½ inch pieces. Boil the Fennel until it is easily pierced with a fork. Pour off water. Melt orange and butter together, then pour over hot Fennel and serve immediately.

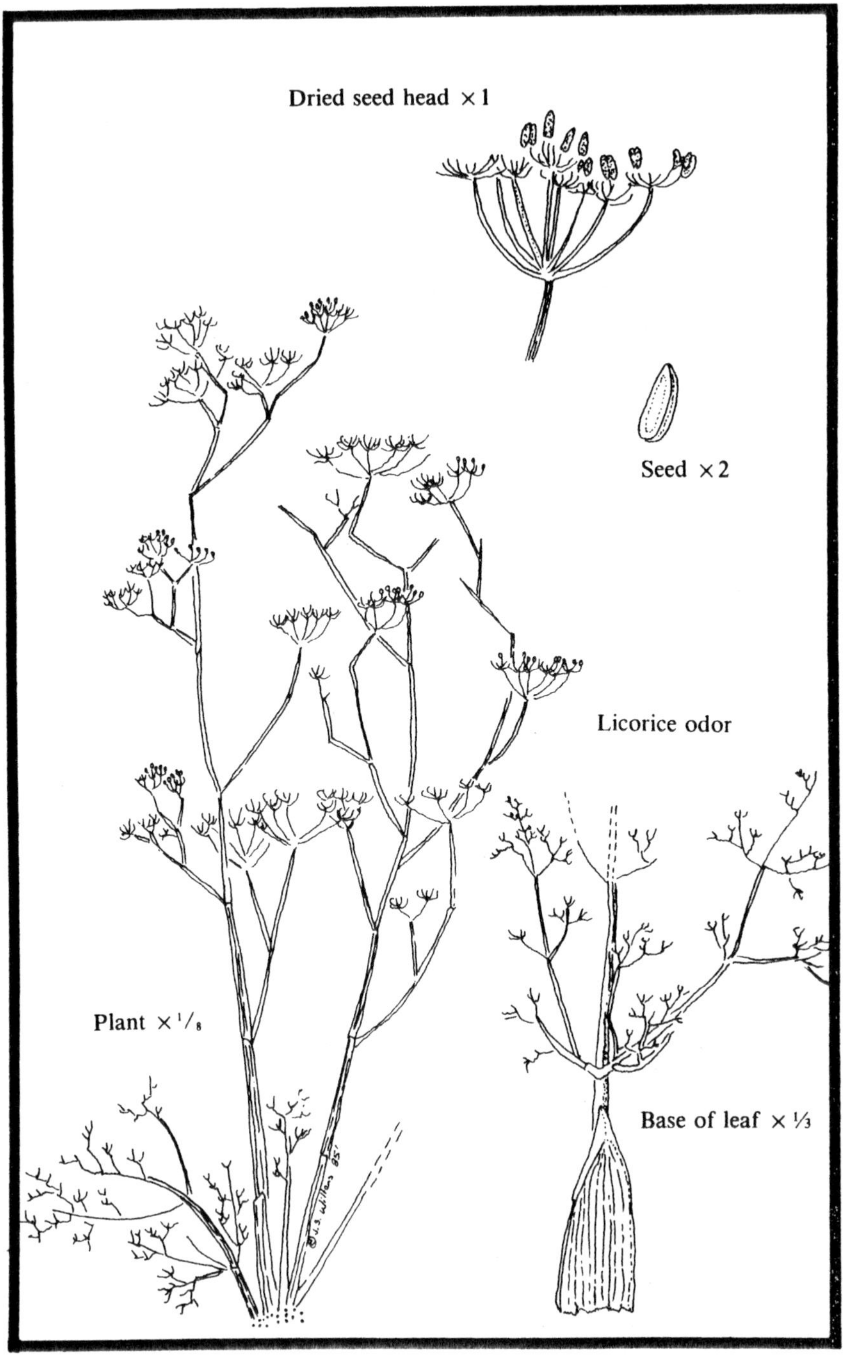

Fennel (*Foeniculum vulgare*)

FENNEL IN TOMATO SAUCE

4 Fennel bulbs (bulbous base at the end of the leaf stalks)
½ cup olive oil
1 onion thinly sliced
2 garlic cloves, minced
1 12 oz. can tomatoes
salt
½ cup dried bread crumbs
½ cup Parmesan cheese
Grated rind of ½ lemon
1 garlic clove, minced

Remove leaves from Fennel, slice thinly. In a skillet, heat oil and add onion and two cloves of minced garlic, sauteing for 2 minutes. Add Fennel and stir fry until Fennel begins to brown. Add tomatoes and season to taste with salt. Over low heat cook four minutes. Transfer Fennel to gratin dish. Combine crumbs, cheese, lemon rind and one clove minced garlic and sprinkle over Fennel. Put under hot broiler for several minutes.

A tea is made by steeping either the leaves or Fennel seeds in hot water.

Commercially, Fennel is used in making licorice flavored candies.

INTERESTING FACTS: Charlemagne was so fond of Fennel that he had it grown on his imperial farms and encouraged its spread through central Europe.

Priests spread Fennel on the floors of early California missions due to the sweet odor emitted when bruised by the feet of the faithful.

Fennel oil has long been used in domestic medicines to help prevent the subject of the lowest form of humor — flatulence (gas in the stomach).

GOOSEBERRIES

Ribes sps.
(Saxifrage Family: Saxifragaceae)

OTHER NAMES: Currants

DESCRIPTION: There are over thirty species of Gooseberries in California, none are known to be poisonous. A shrub with leaves alternate on the stem. In many species the stems bear sharp spines. The common name, Gooseberry, is usually applied to *Ribes* species having stem spines, while the common name, currant, is reserved for the spineless *Ribes* species. Leaves are palmate (with lobes radiating from a central point like the fingers of your hand). Flowers in this genus range in color from yellow to pink to orange to bright red. Ripe berries are oblong to round, often further distinguished by the remains of the withered floral tube attached to one end. The berries may be yellow, red or blue-black, depending on the species. The berry may also be smooth, covered by light bristles or long bristles, again depending on the species.

HABITAT: Along streams, hillsides, open woodlands, washes and ravines.

USES: Spineless berries may be eaten raw after plucking off the floral tube. These berries may also be used in pies and jellies or stored for future use. Berries with bristles or spines should be simmered in a half volume of water to one volume of fruit for thirty minutes and squeezed thru several layers of cheese cloth to obtain a clear juice.

My mother makes a kind of quick jelly she calls Gooseberryioca.

GOOSEBERRYIOCA JELLY

1 cup Gooseberries
1 cup sugar
½ cup water
½ cup water
5 tbsps instant tapioca

Simmer Gooseberries in ½ cup water for thirty minutes, then pass the mixture thru two layers of cheesecloth. Take the other half cup of water and dissolve the sugar and tapioca. Add the Gooseberry juice to the hot tapioca mixture and stir, pour into a jar and allow to cool. Keep stored in the refrigerator.

INTERESTING FACTS: The currant is high in vitamin C and was used in England during WWII to prevent scurvy (a disease associated with inadequate vitamin C in the diet).

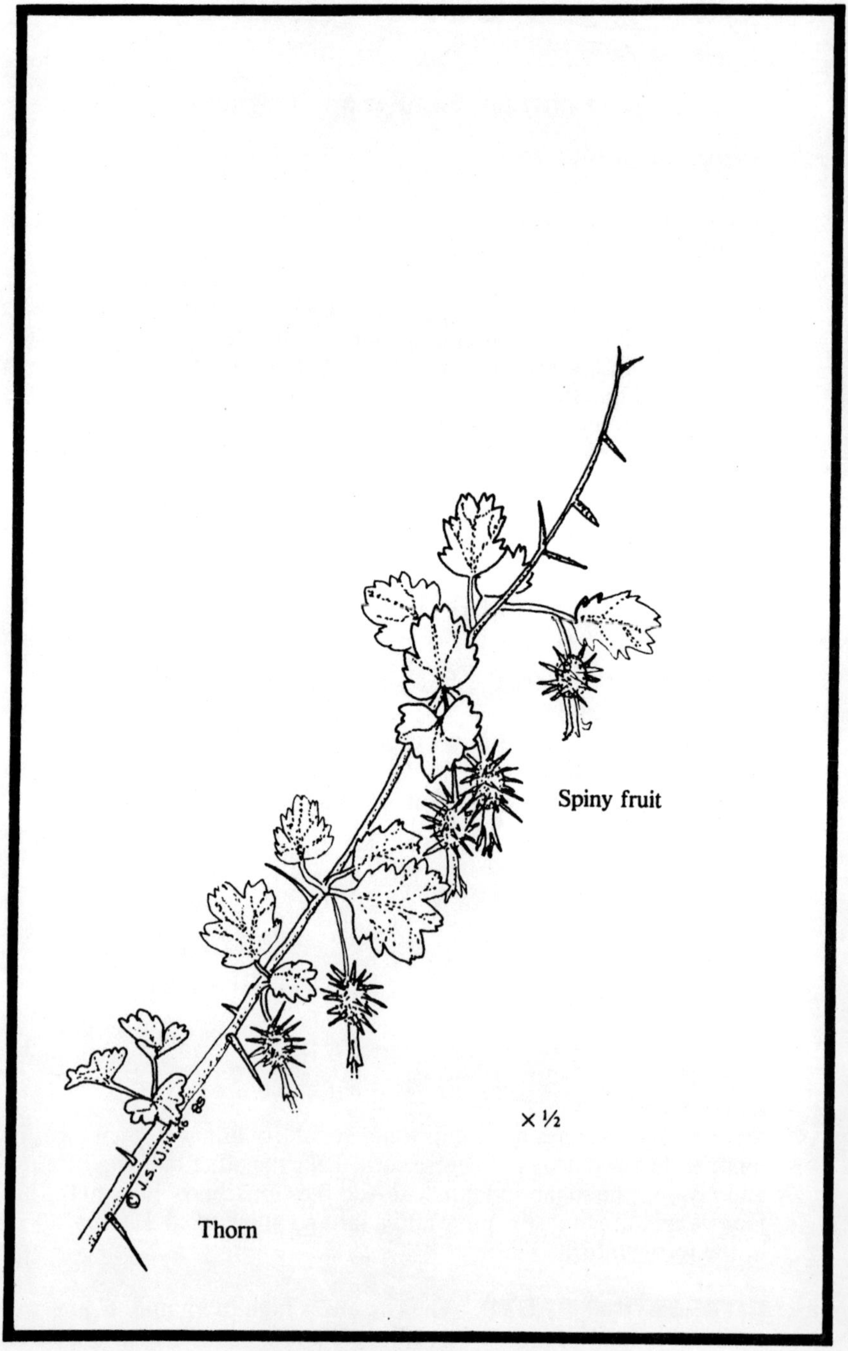

Gooseberry (*Ribes sp.*)

The U.S. Forest Service in California began an eradication program of certain *Ribes* species. It seems that the Gooseberry plant is an intermediate host for a blister rust fungus which attacks species of white pine. It was thought that by destroying the Gooseberry it would break the lifecycle of the fungus. After spending considerable money the Forest Service admitted defeat in trying to remove the tenacious Gooseberry.

GOOSEFOOT

Galium sps.
(Madder Family: Rubiaceae)

OTHER NAMES: Bedstraw, Cleavers

DESCRIPTION: Weak stemmed plant, often using other plants for support. Stem is 4-sided, with downward curving hooklets along the edges. Lance-shaped to spatula-like leaves occur in whorls of 6 to 8. White star shaped flowers are located in the upper axils on slender stalks.

HABITAT: Moist areas, rich woodlands, fields, vacant lots, along streams.

USES: Young plants can be steamed as a potherb. Older plants become too fibrous.

A tea can be made by steeping the dried plant in hot water.

The seeds can be collected and used as a non-caffeine coffee substitute. Roast the seeds in a warm oven (300 degrees F.) until dark brown. Crush and simmer ¾ cup of prepared seeds in a quart of water. Strain and serve.

INTERESTING FACTS: The common name bedstraw comes from the use of this plant as a stuffing material in mattresses. The tiny hooks on the margin of the stem act like Velcro, which helps to keep the plants clumped together in a mattress.

The seeds of sweet scented bedstraw (*Galium triflorum*), contain an anticoagulant (substance that prevents the coagulation of blood). The substance is coumarin, and is present at a concentration of 1 to 3 percent.

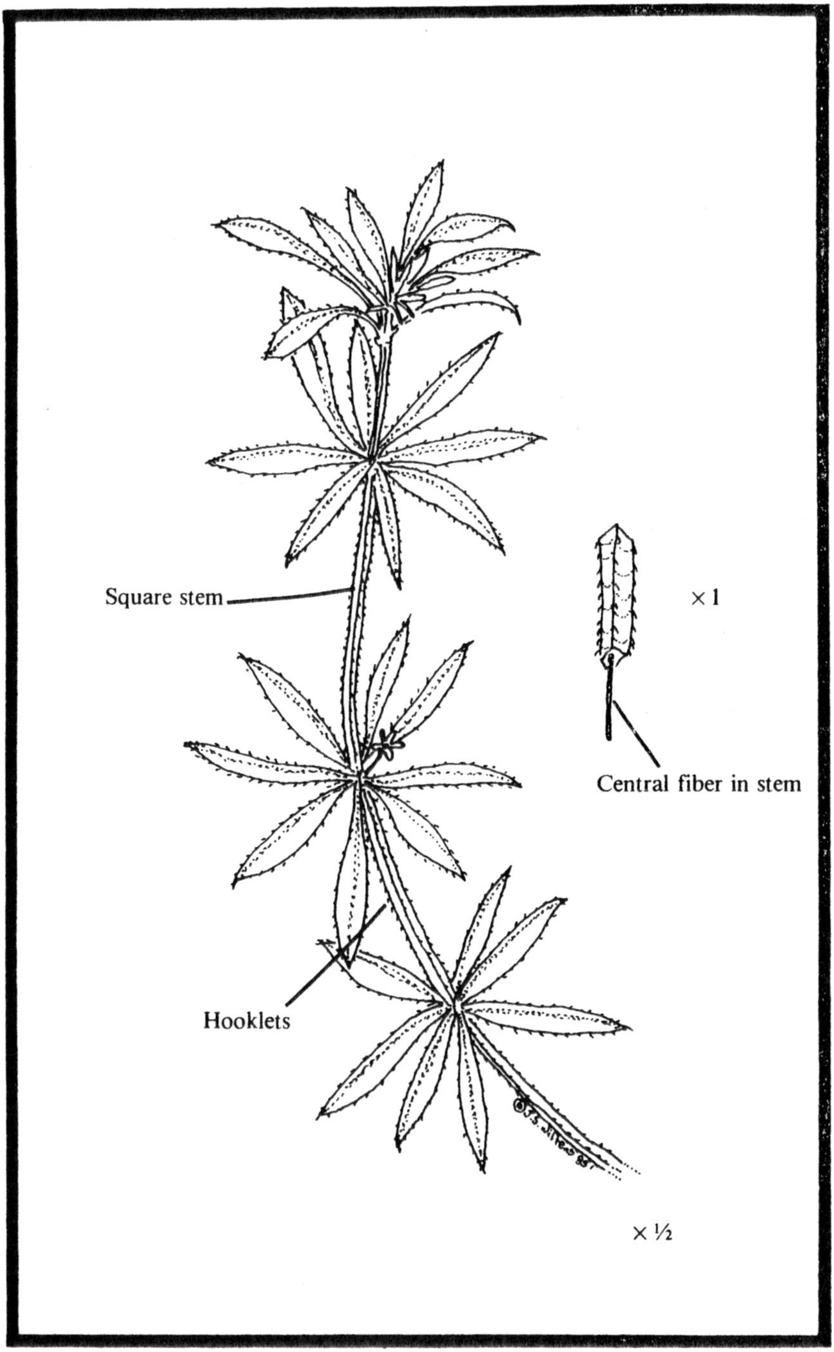

Goosefoot (*Galium sp.*)

HOREHOUND

Marrubium vulgare
(Mint Family: Labiatae)

DESCRIPTION: Erect square stem covered with a white downy hair. Roundish to ovate leaves are wrinkled over entire surface. Petioled leaves are opposite each other. White flowers occur in dense whorls. As the flower stalks dry, a woody stem is left with dried balls that disassociate into the individual seed clusters if disturbed.

HABITAT: Common weed in waste places and fields.

USES: Fresh leaves have a decidedly bitter taste. The leaves can be boiled or dried without losing their bitter flavor. The tea made from these leaves is used for its soothing effect on sore throats.

To make tea, boil a ½ cup fresh leaves (or a ¼ cup dried leaves) in 2 cups of water and sweeten to taste with honey. This is potent stuff and not to everyone's liking.

To make Horehound candy, boil ¼ cup lightly packed fresh herb with 4 cups water. Strain. To each cup hot liquid, add one cup honey and bring to a hard crack (290 degrees), immediately remove and pour onto a buttered cookie sheet. Break into pieces. Store in the refrigerator to keep the candy from sticking together. Although Horehound candy is no longer as popular as it once was, it is still available commercially, primarily at health food stores.

INTERESTING FACTS: The genus name Marrubium is derived from the Hebrew word "marrob" which means bitter juice.

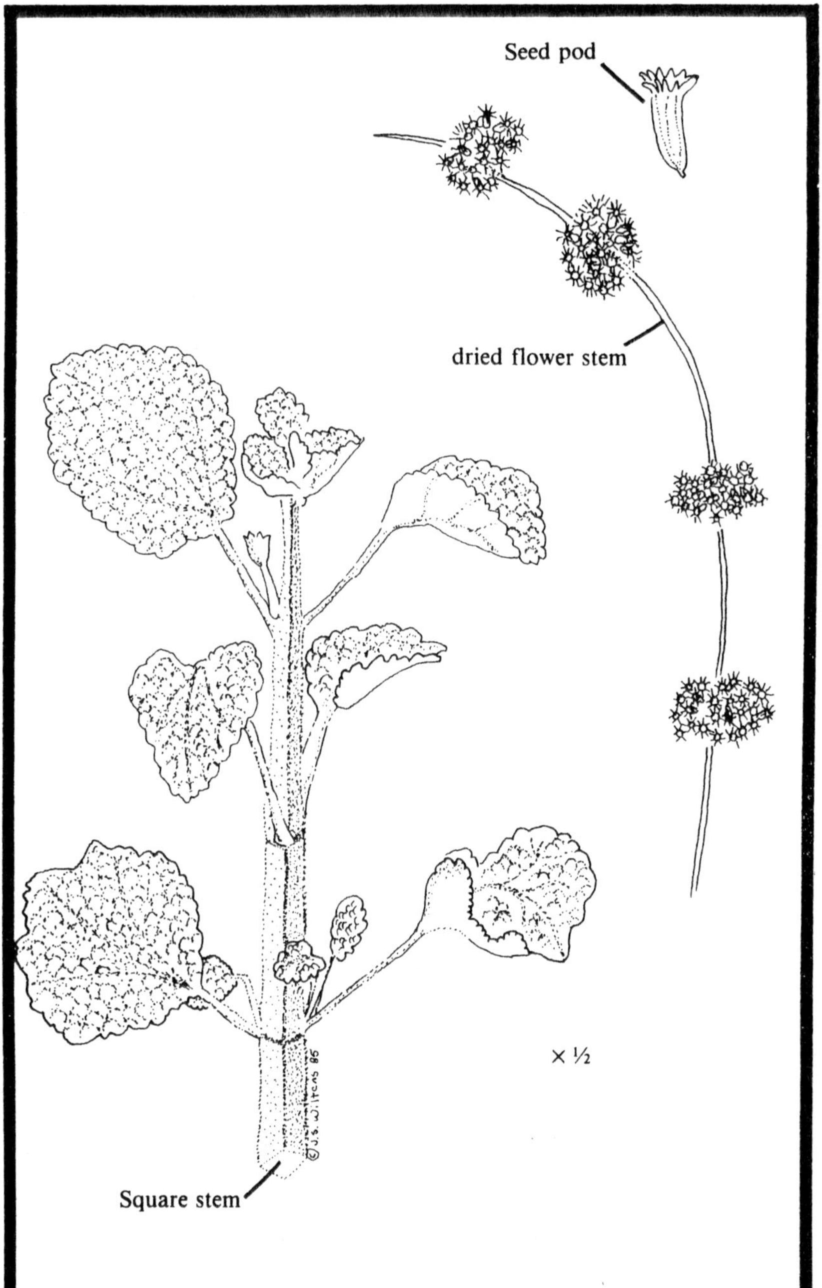

Horehound (*Marrubium vulgare*)

HUCKLEBERRY

Vaccinium ovatum
(Heath Family: Ericaceae)

OTHER NAMES: California Huckleberry

DESCRIPTION: Stout, erect, much branched shrub. Leaves are alternate, with such tight spacing that they have a tendency to overlap. Look closely at the leaf margin and you will see a finely serrated edge. Leaves are a shiny green above (like a holly leaf) and paler beneath. Small white to pink bell-shaped flowers found at leaf axils. Pea-sized berries are dark blue to black with a small collar at the bottom (similar to a blueberry).

People from back East may not recognize this plant as the Huckleberry they are familiar with. That is because it isn't. As so often happens with common names, Huckleberry is the name given to a number of plants. The one you are probably familiar with is in the genus *Gaylussacia.*

HABITAT: Dry forested slopes, along trails.

USES: Raw, cooked or dried. Taste test berries to make sure they are ripe. The berries can be used in muffins, pancakes, jams and other recipes.

To dry berries for storage, put a single layer of berries in the sun for about 10 days with occasional stirring. The berries can also be dried in a warm oven (200 degrees F.) for about 5 hours.

INTERESTING FACTS: Both the blueberry (*V. occidentale*) and the cranberry (*V. macrocarpon*) are found in the Huckleberry genus.

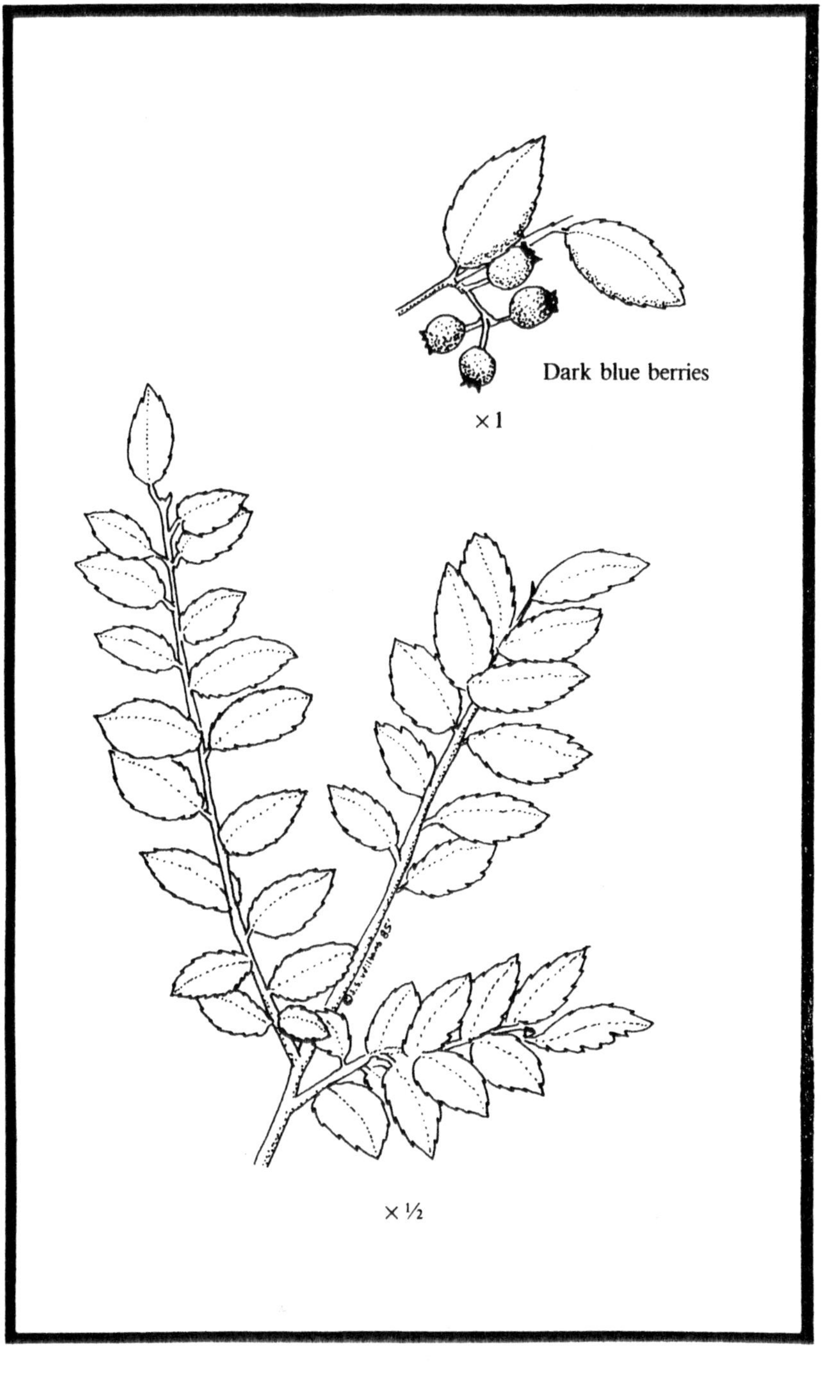

Huckleberry, California (*Vaccinium ovatum*)

MADRONE

Arbutus menziesii
(Heath Family: Ericaceae)

DESCRIPTION: Widely branched tree from 15–120 feet tall. The bark peels readily from the tree exposing a polished red or brown surface. Oval to elliptic leaves are a shiny dark green on top and paler beneath. The leaf margin is finely serrated. Small urn shaped flowers are white to pink. The orange to scarlet berries have a rough textured surface and hang in clusters from the branches.

HABITAT: Wooded slopes and canyons.

USES: The bright red berries seem to be best. Picked raw they may be eaten seeds and all. The taste suggests an apple.

MADRONE SAUCE:

2 cups Madrone berries
sugar
¼ tbsp lemon juice

Place the Madrone berries in a sauce pan and cover with water. Simmer until tender. Pour off the water and blend the berries, seeds, skin and all. Add enough sugar to make it palatable and blend in the lemon juice. Unfortunately the boiling fades the bright red color of the berries.

INTERESTING FACTS: Madrone charcoal was highly prized by the earlier settlers for its use in the manufacture of gunpowder.

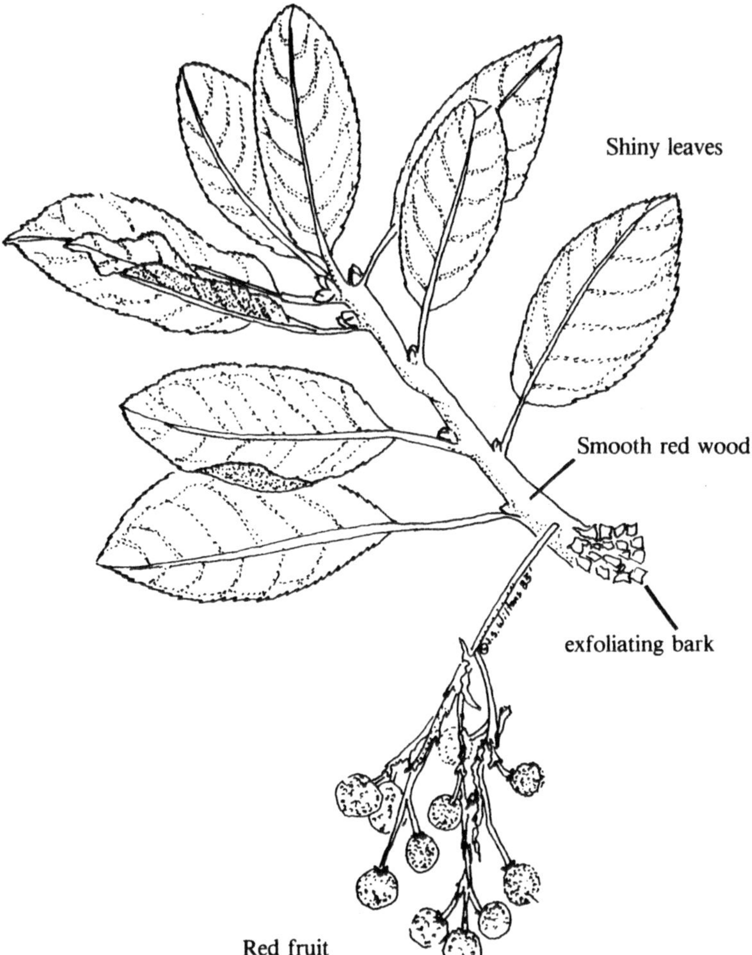

Madrone (*Arbutus menziesii*)

MANZANITA

Arctostaphylos glauca formerly *A. uva-ursi* (Heath Family: Ericaceae)

OTHER NAMES: Bearberry, Bigberry Manzanita

DESCRIPTION: Low growing shrubs to small trees. The sharply upward angled branches have a peeling bark that reveals an attractive smooth red wood underneath. The leathery leaves are the size of a half-dollar. The white to pink urn shaped flowers appear in hanging clusters. The berries look like pea-sized green apples.

HABITAT: Hillsides, sagebrush areas, prefers dry rocky soil.

USES: There are over 40 species of Manzanita in California and it is easy to confuse one species with another. One thing is certain though, the edibility of the fruits varies greatly from one plant to another. In searching the literature I found a number of references which suggested that all Manzanita species were equally palatable. Acting as my own guinea pig, I've sampled raw fruits at different stages of growth from a variety of species and had to spit them out, they were so astringent. Ignoring the raw taste test, I've tried boiling some berries into a Manzanita cider and my parents declared that even though I hadn't discovered a replacement for orange juice, I had made progress towards something that would dissolve tooth enamel. It is probably the presence of high quantities of tannic acid that render some species inedible.

The palatable species have a somewhat sweet taste when raw with little astringency. These can be eaten fresh off the branch, spitting out the granite hard seeds. Don't eat too many though, as they have a laxative effect.

A refreshing cider can be made from the berries of *A. glauca*:

MANZANITA CIDER

1 cup reddish Manzanita berries
2 tbsps honey
2 cups water

Pick the persistent stems off the berries and place berries in a sauce pan. Simmer for 20 minutes. Add the honey. Lightly crush the berries and leave overnight. The following day, decant the liquid, chill and serve.

INTERESTING FACTS: The volatile gases given off by Manzanita when it burns make for an extremely hot fire. People who own wood

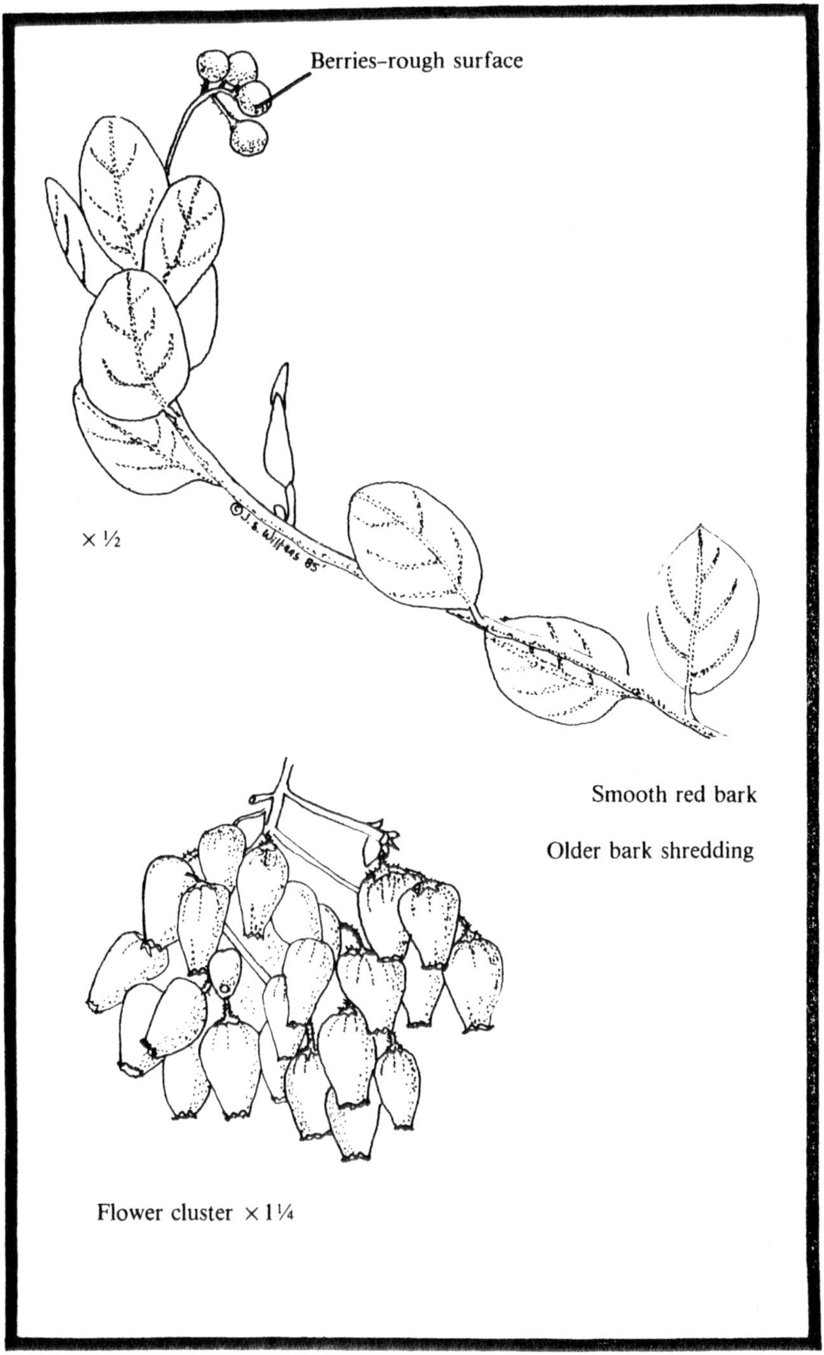

Manzanita, bigberry (*Arctostaphylos glauca*)

stoves are cautioned not to use Manzanita logs for a fire because they burn so hot they can actually melt a cast iron stove.

The burl stump at the bases of some species of Manzanita is quite resistant to forest fires. While the surface branches may be destroyed by fire, the burl will propagate new shoots a short time later.

California Indians probably did not start smoking until their contact with the white man. But when the habit arrived they quickly looked for a substitute source for hard to obtain tobacco. The leaves from *Arctostaphylos uva-ursi* provided their first home grown smoking tobacco.

MINER'S LETTUCE

Montia perfoliata
(Purslane Family: Portulacaceae)

OTHER NAMES: Indian Lettuce

DESCRIPTION: An upright succulent annual. Leaves arise from a basal clump, with a thin fibrous root system. Some leaves have the shape of a serpent's head or a half round outline. The most distinctive feature is the presence of round leaves with a flowering raceme seemingly coming through the center of the leaf. The tiny white flowers have 5 petals. Fruits contain 1-3 shiny black seeds.

HABITAT: Moist sites, often growing in the shade of trees, around springs, meadows.

USES: Gather fresh leaves and stalks for use in salads. Merely chop the freshly gathered plant into bite size pieces, add a little oil and vinegar and you have an excellent salad.

Miner's Lettuce can also be used as a spinach substitute, requiring several minutes of steaming. This plant is also quite good stir fried. The following is one of my favorite recipes:

WILTED MINER'S LETTUCE SALAD

¾ to 1 lb. Miner's Lettuce
5 green onions, thinly sliced
2 hard cooked eggs, chopped
1 raw egg
2 tbsps each, sugar, white wine vinegar and red wine vinegar
½ lb. sliced bacon, cut into ½'' pieces

Beat raw egg with sugar, white vinegar and red vinegar and set aside.

In a large frying pan, cook bacon until crisp. Remove bacon pieces and drain. Discard all but 3 tbsps. drippings from pan. Stirring constantly with whisk, slowly pour egg-vinegar mix into warm bacon drippings: cook until mix thickens slightly (approx. 1 minute). Immediately add Miner's Lettuce and stir, coating each leaf (approx. 1 minute). Add chopped eggs and serve.

INTERESTING FACTS: During the gold rush in California the miners were often without fresh vegetables. Following the Indians' example, the miners gathered *Montia sps.* to round out their diet. Thus the common name, Miner's Lettuce. Due to the high Vitamin C content of this plant, early settlers recognized it as a preventive or cure for scurvy.

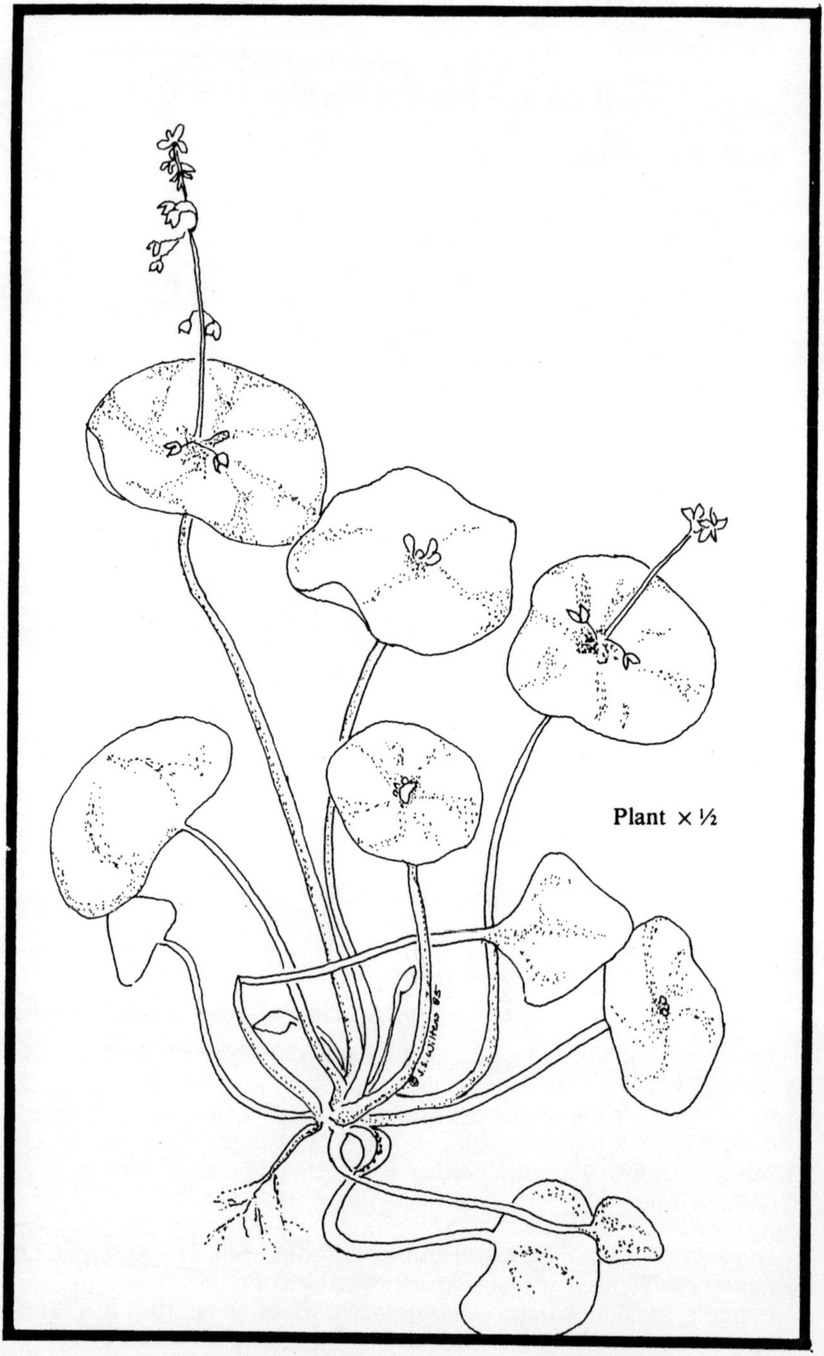

Miner's Lettuce (*Montia perfoliata*)

MOUNTAIN GRAPE

Berberis pinnata formerly ***Mahonia pinnata***
(Barberry Family: Berberidaceae)

OTHER NAMES: Barberry

DESCRIPTION: Shrub with stiff erect branches. Oval glossy green leaves with spikelets along the leaf margin (very similar to holly leaves). Small yellow flowers occur in long terminal clusters at the end of stems. Berries are blue with a grayish waxy coating. If you strip away some bark, the wood is yellow underneath.

HABITAT: Rocky slopes, pine forests, sometimes planted as a native garden ornamental.

USES: California Indians used to eat the berries raw, I find my over-civilized palate prefers them with a little sugar, due to their sourness.

Try crushing a quarter cup of berries in a quart of water, strain, add honey to taste, chill and serve.

To make Mountain Grape jelly:

MOUNTAIN GRAPE JELLY

4 cups Mountain Grapes
4 cups sugar

Place berries in a sauce pan and mash. Heat berry mush to boiling. Pass berry juice through a cheesecloth bag, squeezing out the juice. Add sugar to juice and boil with gentle heat while covered for about 30 minutes. Pour jelly into jars and store in the refrigerator. (Mountain Grapes are naturally tart and high in pectin, which is the reason you don't add lemon and pectin as called for in most jelly recipes).

INTERESTING FACTS: The root of Mountain Grape contains a yellow crystalline alkaloid, berberine. The Indians used to boil the root to make a yellow dye.

The yellow wood was once carved into the crucifixes worn by Spanish-Americans.

An eradication program was instigated against Mountain Grape in wheat growing areas. Mountain Grape serves as an intermediate host for black wheat stem rust. Without Mountain Grape, the fungus cannot form spores which infect wheat crops.

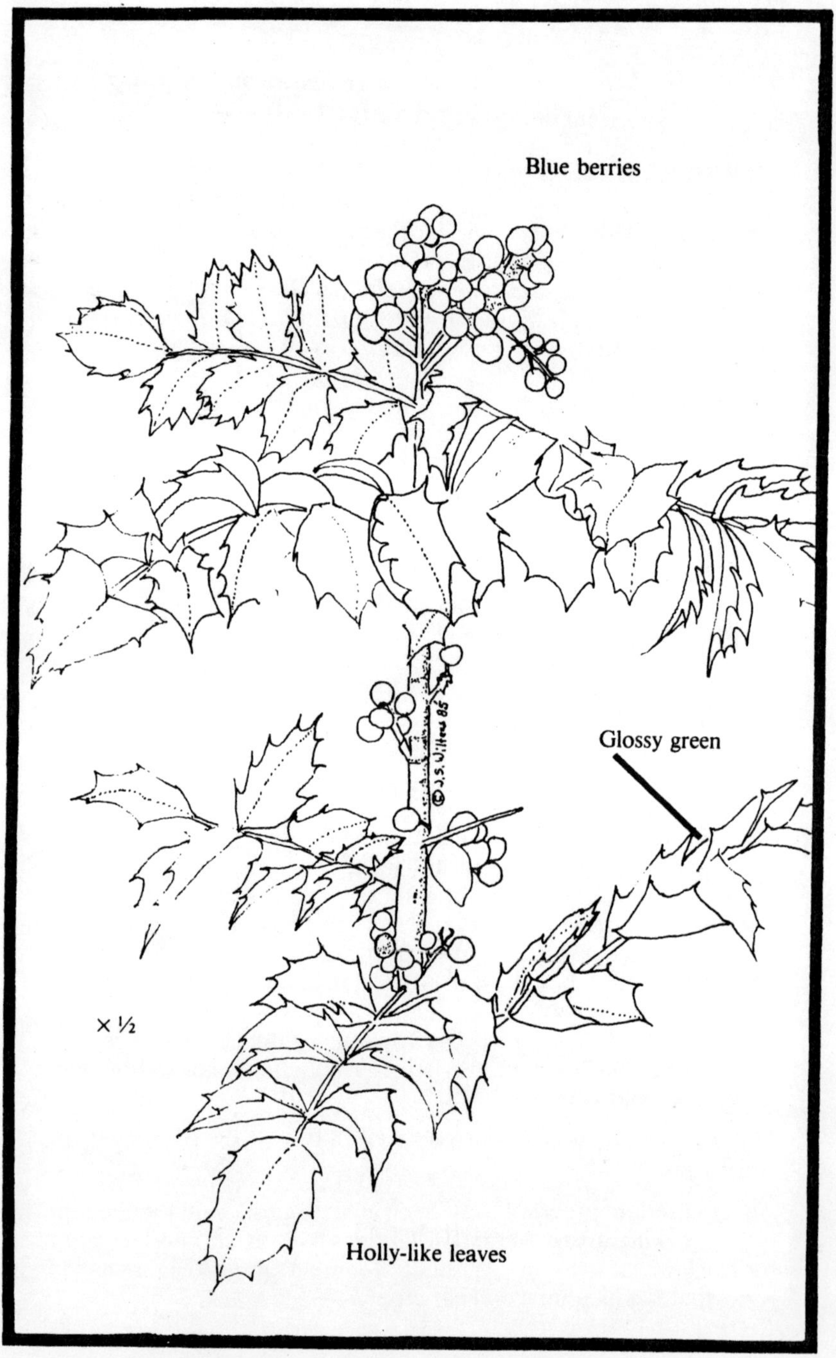

Mountain Grape (*Berberis pinnata*)

MUSTARD

Brassica sps.
(Mustard Family: Cruciferae)

DESCRIPTION: Erect, freely branching stems. The lower leaves are pinnatifid (cleft into narrow lobes not reaching to the midrib), while the upper leaves may have a toothed or smooth margin. Bright sulphur yellow flowers in elongated clusters. Flowers have 4 petals and 4 long and two short anthers. Slender seed pods contain the pinhead size seeds.

HABITAT: Hillsides, waste areas, vacant lots, recently plowed fields and orchards.

USES: The leaves, flower pods and seeds may all be used. Pick leaves early and use raw in salads. Chop the leaves finely and mix with other salad greens that need some spicing up.

Older leaves may be boiled for 20 minutes and served like spinach.

The unopened flower heads at the end of the stems may be added raw to a salad or boiled and served like tiny broccoli. Boil for about 3 minutes, until they turn a bright green.

To collect the seeds, wait until the pods dry to a parchment yellow. Strip the pods from the stems into a grocery bag. To remove the seeds from the pods, either sun dry or put them in a warm oven. When the pods are beginning to split open to reveal the seeds, transfer several handfuls to a sturdy bag. For small amounts, we put on leather gloves and rub the pods between our hands briskly. The rubbing action breaks the pods open, releasing the BB-sized seeds. A coarse sieve is used to separate the seeds from the chaff.

MUSTARD SPREAD

½ cup Mustard seeds
½ cup flour
wine vinegar

Grind the Mustard seeds with a mortar and pestle or in a food processor. Spread flour in a large cake pan and place under the oven broiler, stirring the flour regularly so it browns evenly. Remove the flour and mix with the ground Mustard powder. Mix vinegar and water, half and half. Add enough vinegar-water to the Mustard flour combination to get the proper consistency.

INTERESTING FACTS: The prevalence of Mustard in California is partly due to the early priests. When traveling between missions they would spread Mustard seed to mark the trail. Sort of a "golden pathway to God".

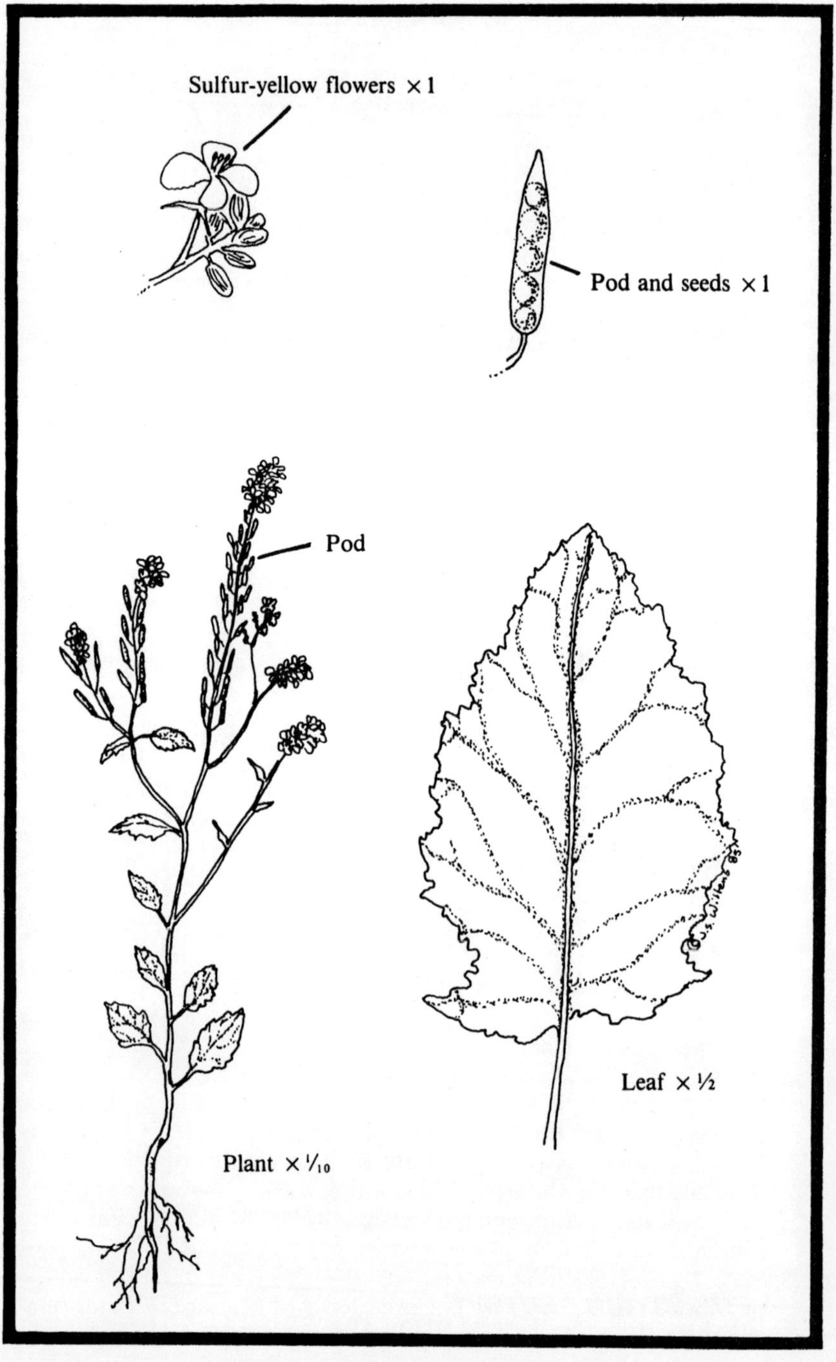

Mustard (Brassica sp.)

The early settlers often used Mustard plasters to relieve congestion. To make a Mustard plaster, add one part finely ground Mustard seed to one part flour. Add sufficient water to make a paste. Spread this paste over some cheese cloth or muslim and cover with another piece of cloth. This plaster was then applied to the chest.

Mustard is an example of a plant that if eaten in excessive quantities could be harmful. The zippy taste in Mustard is due to irritant oils, glycoside isothiocyanates. If animals are fed on large quantities of grain containing Mustard seeds they can become quite ill. Like many things in life, it should be enjoyed in reasonable quantities.

OAK

Quercus sps.
(Beech Family: Fagaceae)

DESCRIPTION: There are 300 species of Oak that range from massive trees to waist high shrubs. Two species in California, the Coast Live Oak (*Quercus agrifolia*) and the Valley Oak (*Quercus lobata*) were the preferred species among the native California Indians (though other Oaks may be used similarly, (ie. *Q. ilex and Q. douglasii*). The species mentioned are tall open crowned trees. Leaves are alternate on the twigs and among the species go from oval toothed leaves the size of a half dollar to large flexible leaves with rounded margins. The acorn is the most distinctive feature, a nutlet with a scaled turban cap.

HABITAT: Foothills, dry open woodland.

CAUTION: ***The presence of tannic acid (the same substance found in high concentrations in redwood bark) makes it unwise to eat large quantities of unleached acorns. The tannic acid has a cumulative effect which could cause kidney damage.***

USES: California Indians relied heavily on the acorn as a major food staple. But the preparation phase is very important to make this food palatable.

As a child I found out early on that certain types of Oak nuts had a sweetish taste when eaten raw. I would pop the acorn nut out of the shell and crack the nut between my teeth. The initial nut meat taste was pleasant, but, as I chewed, this sweet taste was replaced with a bitter almost metallic aftertaste. Taste-testing a few nuts is harmless, but trying to consume large quantities of unleached nuts could be damaging. The nut meats are rendered safe in the following manner.

Dehull several pounds of acorns. Chop the nut meat finely or grind in a food processor (the Indians originally ground the nuts with a pestle on a flat rock). Water must then be passed repeatedly through the meal to remove the bitter tannin. One method is to put the meal into a tightly woven sack such as a pillow case, set this in a colander and allow water to run over the bag with occasional kneading. This process takes many hours. If you are fortunate to have a nearby spring, you can set the bag of meal under a flowing spigot from the spring. A unique method of leaching is to suspend the bag in the water holding tank of a toilet and let the natural flushing action work its magic. To tell if the leaching process is complete, taste-test the meal at intervals to see if the bitter taste is removed.

Another leaching method is to boil (approximately 2 hours) the shelled acorns, changing the water each time it becomes brown. The taste test will tell you when the process is complete.

Q. agrifolia × ¾

Coast live oak

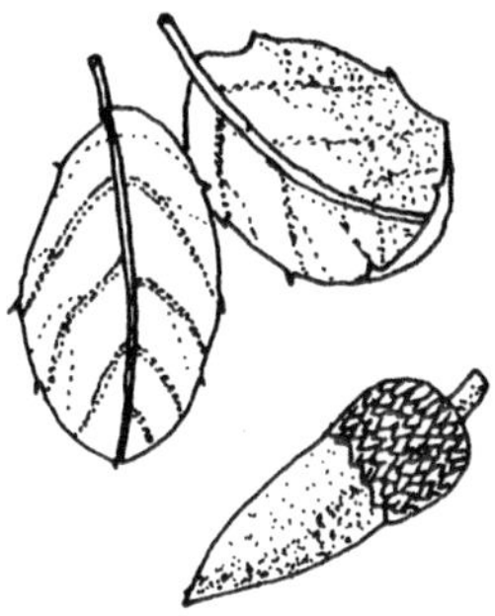

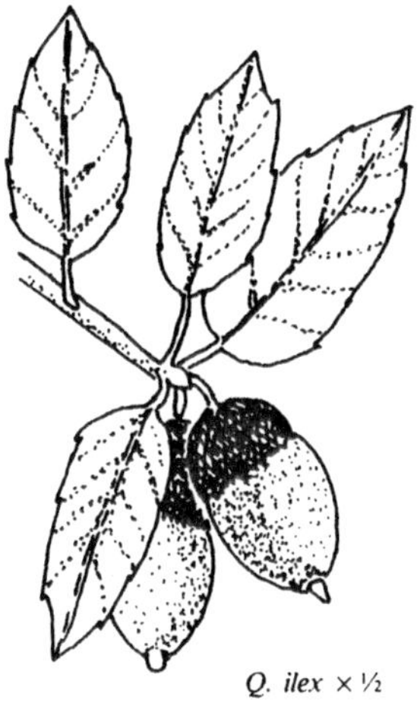

Q. ilex × ½

Holly oak

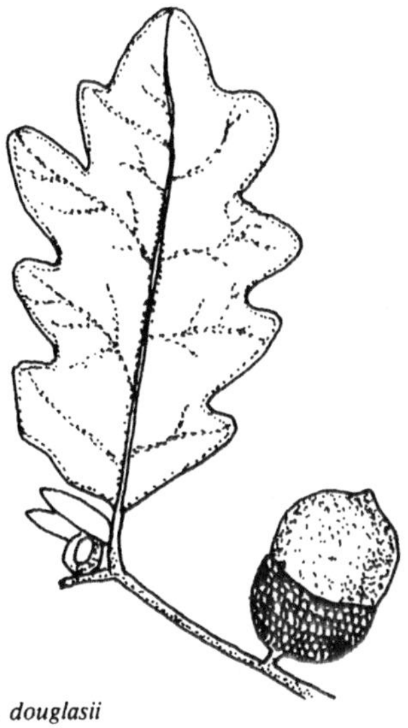

Q. douglasii

Blue oak

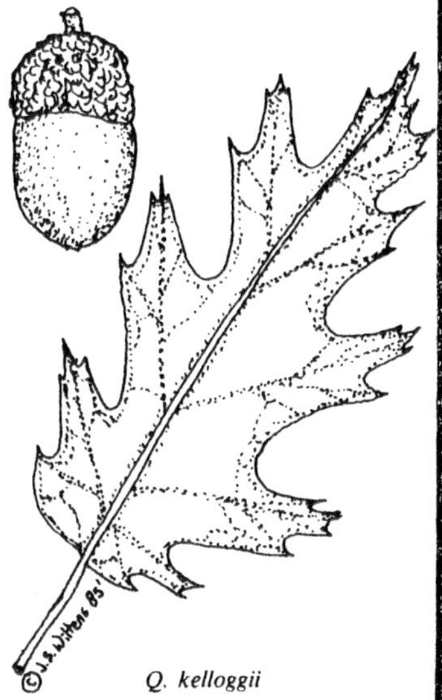

Q. kelloggii

Calif. black oak

Oak (*Quercus sps.*)

The leached meal is then dried for future use. To make a civilized acorn bread:

OAK BREAD

1 cup leached acorn meal
½ cup cornmeal
½ cup whole wheat flour
3 tblsps salad oil
1 tsp salt
1 tblsp baking powder
¼ cup honey
1 egg
1 cup milk

Combine acorn meal, cornmeal, wheat flour, salt and baking powder. In a separate bowl combine honey, egg and milk. Mix the contents of both bowls together and pour into a greased 8 × 8 inch pan and bake at 350 degrees for 25 minutes.

INTERESTING FACTS: An analysis of leached acorn meal shows 62% carbohydrate, 5% protein and 20% fat. This compares to wheat flour with 75% carbohydrates, 11% protein and 1% fat.

The California Indians were thought to have developed a rather sedentary life-style due to the large abundance of a stable food source as represented by the Oak. The Oak was so vital that good groves were owned by families and warfare could result if a tribe gathered acorns in a grove without permission.

To leach the tannic acid from acorn meal, California Indians would scoop a depression in the sand. To this depression they would add the mashed acorns. For a period of hours they would pour water over the meal to leach out the tannins. The sand was not always completely removed from the meal, which, over years of eating acorn mush, would take its toll. Older California Indians had badly worn teeth from the abrasive action of the sand, and bad teeth were a contributing cause of death in the Indian populace.

Tannic acid is one of the ingredients used in tanning skins to make leather. The Oak tree has long been the source of tannin. The tannin combines with the protein in skins and helps the finished leather to resist decay and remain pliable.

OATS, WILD

Avena fatua
(Grass Family: Gramineae)

DESCRIPTION: Grass growing to waist height. Parallel venation in both leaves and stems, a characteristic of all grasses. The flowering structure occurs at the end of the leaf stem, horizontal branchlets support the flower spikelets. The flower has two scales or bractlets covering it with a twisted or bent bristle extending from the rear. If you strip a spikelet of its outer sheath, you will discover the grain, a soft white starchy liquid in its early stages, hardening with age.

HABITAT: Open areas, empty lots, roadsides, fields.

CAUTION: ***Only grain that is green or golden should be picked. If it is blackened by a fuzzy mold or black spikelets, it may be contaminated with ergot. Ergot is a fungus (Claviceps purpurea) which, during the Middle Ages, was associated with a disease called "St. Anthony's Fire." Whole villages would be driven to madness or death by the consumption of ergot contaminated grain in bread. Sufferers of the disease would often lose limbs due to vascular constriction. Recent work on ergot has shown it to contain a number of toxic alkaloids; one of its well known constituents is lysergic acid, a precursor for the hallucinogen LSD.***

USES: After going through this process, I have a lot more respect for a lowly box of oatmeal.

Collect the seed heads in the transition stage from green to golden. Merely pull your hand up the length of the stem, maybe you remember doing this as a child to obtain the little rockets which were thrown with great relish at friends wearing wool sweaters (for those showered by oat rockets, it was annoyingly difficult to remove the tenacious oat seeds from your back).

Spread the grain on a plastic sheet in the sun. The drying process should take several days. Place a thin layer, about ½ inch thick, of Oats on a wire mesh screen and pass it over a fire, shaking vigorously. Don't hold it so close to the fire that the grain ignites. This will burn off the stiff bristles on the oat grain. Winnow the chaff from the Oats. Grind the resultant product and pass through a flour sifter which will remove any left over chaff. The resultant meal can be used in making bread, or better yet, oatmeal cookies.

INTERESTING FACTS: Oats were not originally found in the Americas. They were probably an import brought over by the Spanish.

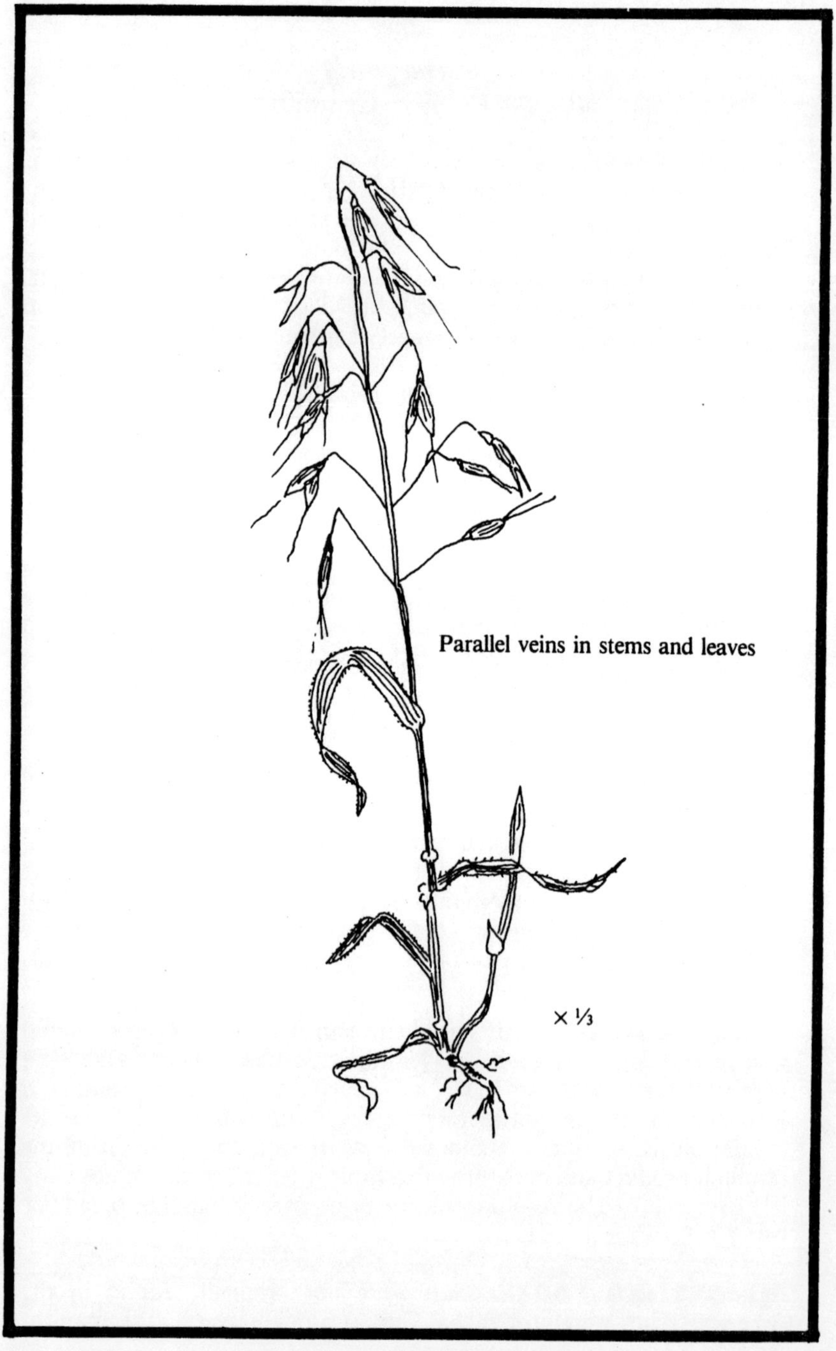

Oats, Wild (*Avena sp.*)

OXALIS

Oxalis sps.
(Wood Sorrel Family: Oxalidaceae)

OTHER NAMES: Shamrock, Sour Grass, Sorrel

DESCRIPTION: Perennial. The clover shaped leaves cap a thin stem which rises from a wiry rootstock. Bright 5 petaled yellow flowers occur in groups at the end of a succulent stalk. Flowers of other species may be purple, red or white. During the evening and early morning, the leaves fold down and the flowers curl into a closed tube.

HABITAT: Open sunny areas, often invades planting borders and roadway dividers.

CAUTION: ***Calcium in blood precipitates with oxalic acid to form insoluble calcium oxalates. Eating large quantities of oxalate containing plants has led to death in livestock and man.***

Since Oxalis contains oxalates, I would recommend restricting intake to reasonable quantities. Children have been known to become nauseous after consuming several handfuls of Oxalis stems.

USES: The tart lemony tang makes the stalks good for a trailside nibble. The stalks may also be diced and added as a salad garnish.

Oregon settlers are said to have used this plant as a rhubarb substitute for making pies. I have a reservation about consuming large quantities of Oxalis due to its oxalic acid content.

INTERESTING FACTS: The genus name is derived from the Greek, "oxus", meaning "sharp" or "sour". The sour taste is due to soluble forms of oxalic acid, a chemical found in many plants, such as spinach, beet tops and rhubarb.

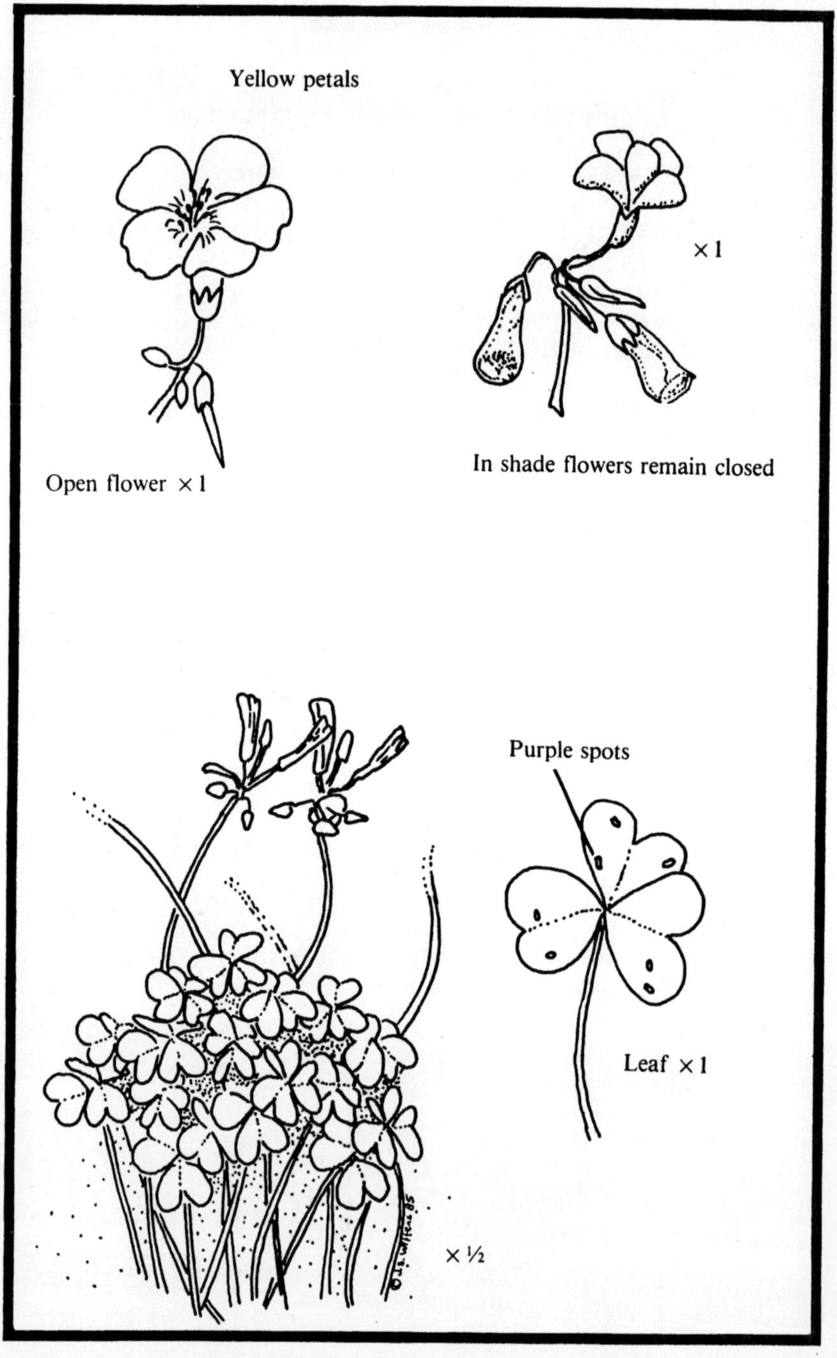

Oxalis (*Oxalis sp.*)

PINE, DIGGER

Pinus sabiniana
(Pine Family: Pinaceae)

DESCRIPTION: The Digger Pine can grow up to 90 feet high, but is more commonly found between 30 and 50 feet in height. A rangy opencrowned tree with needles in clusters of three. Foliage is a dull grey green. The pineapple size cones have thick scales with downwardly projecting hooks. Unlike their more stately Pine relatives, Digger Pines are often found growing at a tilted angle, which makes them obvious at a distance.

HABITAT: Dry foothills, open sagebrush areas.

USES: Many species of Pines have edible nuts, so what is said here concerning the Digger Pine will apply to other Pines as well. The nut of the Digger Pine is fairly large compared to other Pine species, so the effort involved in collecting Digger nuts is better rewarded. The winged nuts are found sandwiched between the scales of the Pine cone. The nuts are best obtained from cones that are still green with the scales tightly sealed or only slightly parted. Since the cones usually remain on the tree until they have opened and dispersed their seeds, you need a method for collecting ripe cones. You might try knocking cones from a tree with a long pole or maybe you are agile enough to hoist yourself up with the aid of lower branches (Digger Pine wood is notoriously brittle, so use common sense). My preferred technique is to look at the base of trees in early autumn when squirrels are busy downing cones for their own supplies. The cones should be handled carefully to avoid a cut from the taloned scales.

The nuts are wedged back between the sealed scales. To remove the nuts from a green cone, place the cone next to a heat source, such as a campfire. You can wrap the cone in some aluminum foil and bury it in the coals like a hot potato or merely prop it up in front of the fire. Either way, make sure the scales do not ignite. As the cone dries, the scales will lift open exposing the seeds. Pounding lightly on a rock will dislodge the nuts. Crack the nut with a rock or strong teeth and remove the nut meat.

In a real survival situation, the cambium layer just behind the bark can act as food. You need to make a slit in the tree with an ax and peel back the bark. Wtih the bark removed a thin layer of cells called the cambium is exposed. The cambium can be scratched away from the tree with a fingernail and eaten fresh. The texture is mucilaginous and slightly sweet. I admit that it would have to be a survival situation to

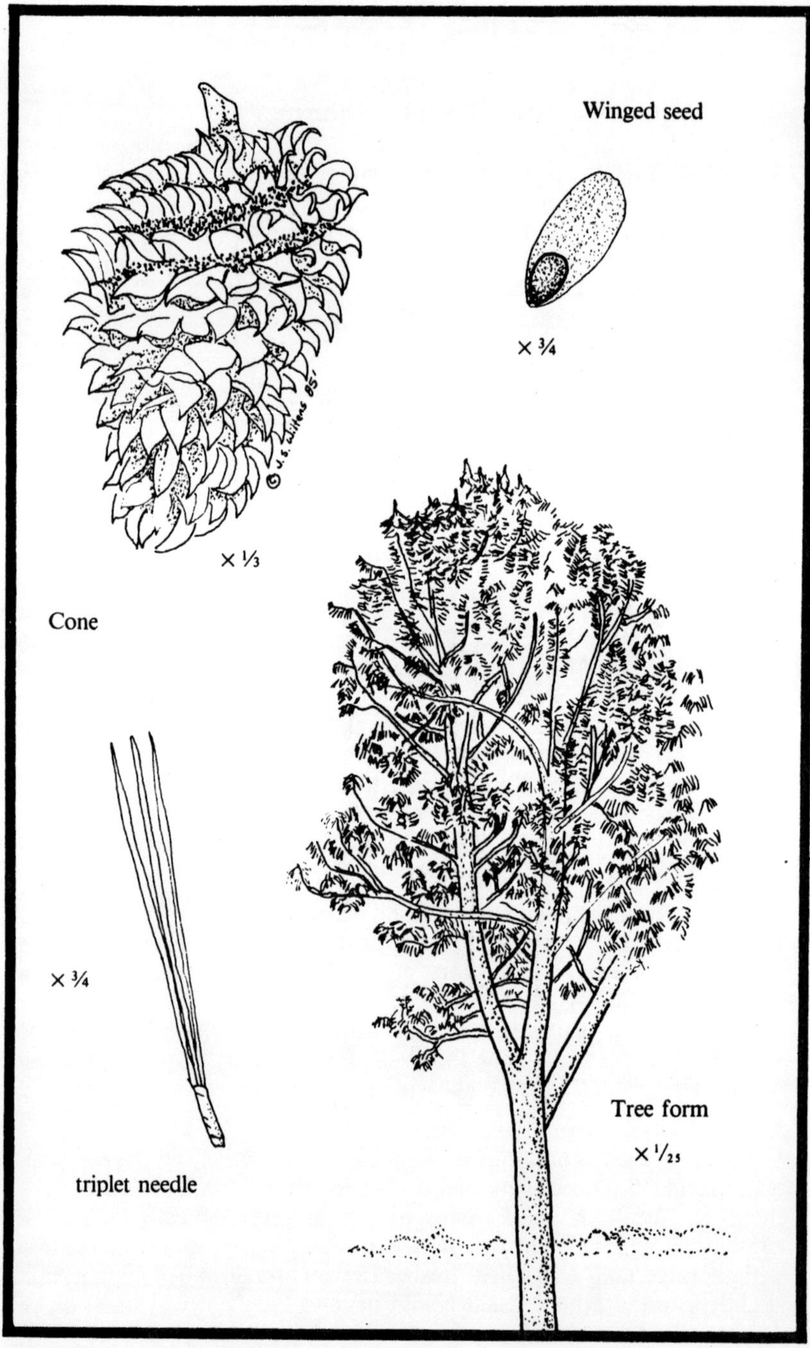

Digger Pine (*Pinus sabiniana*)

force me to rely on eating large quantities of cambium. The slight turpentine taste of the cambium makes it objectionable to most civilized palates. During the autumn when I am felling lumber for the fireplace, I find that a small ball of the fresh cambium chewed like gum is not at all unpleasant. In this case my preferred species of Pine is the Lodge Pole Pine (*Pinus murrayana*). If you do strip off the cambium layer, understand that this will kill the entire tree.

Pine needles are high in vitamin C. An analysis of White Pine (*Pinus strobus*) shows the needles to contain 5 times as much vitamin C as lemons. A tea made from fresh needles and sweetened with honey is both healthful and a pleasant taste of nature.

If you find a nodule of fresh Pine sap, try chewing it like gum. My favorite species of Pine for Pine sap gum is the Jeffrey Pine (*Pinus jeffreyi*). It has a pleasant pineapple smell, which distinguishes it from other Pines. Make sure that the resin is very fresh. Older resin is not translucent. Any crystallization in the resin suggest it is too old to make gum out of. If you try older resin it will leave a very unpleasant aftertaste that takes hours to get rid of.

INTERESTING FACTS: The growth habit of the Digger Pine is much different from its forest relatives. The stereotyped forest Pine with its upright posture, dense needles and wedge shaped form is an adaptation for optimum use of light. The Digger Pine, on the other hand, rarely grows in dense stands. Instead, it has adapted to arid conditions by having a minimal number of needles, and these are grey-green to retard excessive heating of the needle during the hot dry summer months.

PLANTAIN

Plantago lanceolata and *major*
(Plantain Family: Plantaginaceae)

OTHER NAMES: Common Plantain, English Plantain

DESCRIPTION: The roundish (*P. major*) to somewhat lanceolate (*P. lanceolata*) shaped leaves originate at the base of the plant. Leaves are distinctly ribbed with parallel veins. The flower heads are borne at the end of a narrrow leafless stalk that rises above the leaves. The flowers are tightly packed on a cone to cylindrical shaped structure at the end of the flower stalk. For the most part, the greenish to purplish flowers are rather inconspicuous.

HABITAT: Waste areas, roadsides, vacant lots.

USES: Pick the young green leaves before the flower stalks have elongated beyond the leaves. Chop the leaves and steam for 10 minutes, serve with butter. If you pick the leaves when they are too old you won't need any dental floss after the meal. The long fibers will make your teeth work overtime.

INTERESTING FACTS: This plant was not indigenous to North America but was a native of the Old World. The Indians called this plant "white man's footsteps", due to its almost simultaneous appearance with the settlers' homesteads.

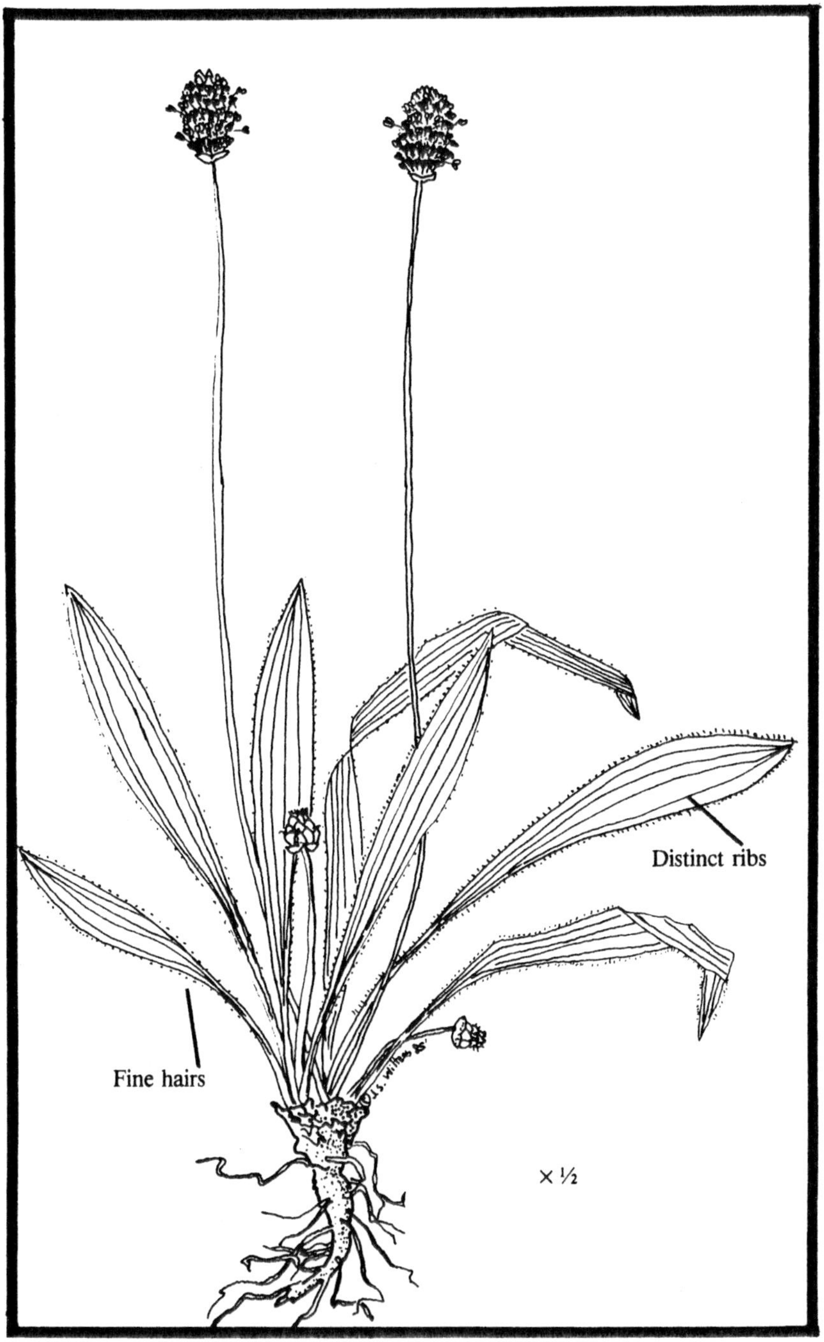

Plantain (*Plantago lanceolata*)

PRICKLY LETTUCE

Lactuca serriola
(Sunflower Family: Compositae)

OTHER NAMES: Wild Lettuce

DESCRIPTION: Usually a single unbranched stem covered with bristly spines. Leaves usually clasp stem and have a club shaped outline. The margin of the leaves is rough and jagged. A distinguishing characteristic is a row of prickles along the main vein on the underside of the leaf. Yellow flowers are similar to dandelion, but a number of flowers are spaced up a flower stalk. If you break the stem or a leaf it will ooze a milky sap.

HABITAT: Waste areas, vacant lots, fields and roadsides.

USES: The young leaves, which may be distinguished from other plants by the row of prickles on the main vein, may be used raw in salads. I find even the young plants to be too bitter for my taste, and prefer the plants boiled for 15 minutes in a little salted water. The older plants will require several boilings to be made palatable.

INTERESTING FACTS: The genus name Lactuca is derived from the Latin "lac" for milk, due to the milky sap that exudes from the broken stems.

Supposedly the milky sap from this plant has been collected in a manner similar to the way the juice is collected from the opium poppy and used as a mild form of opium.

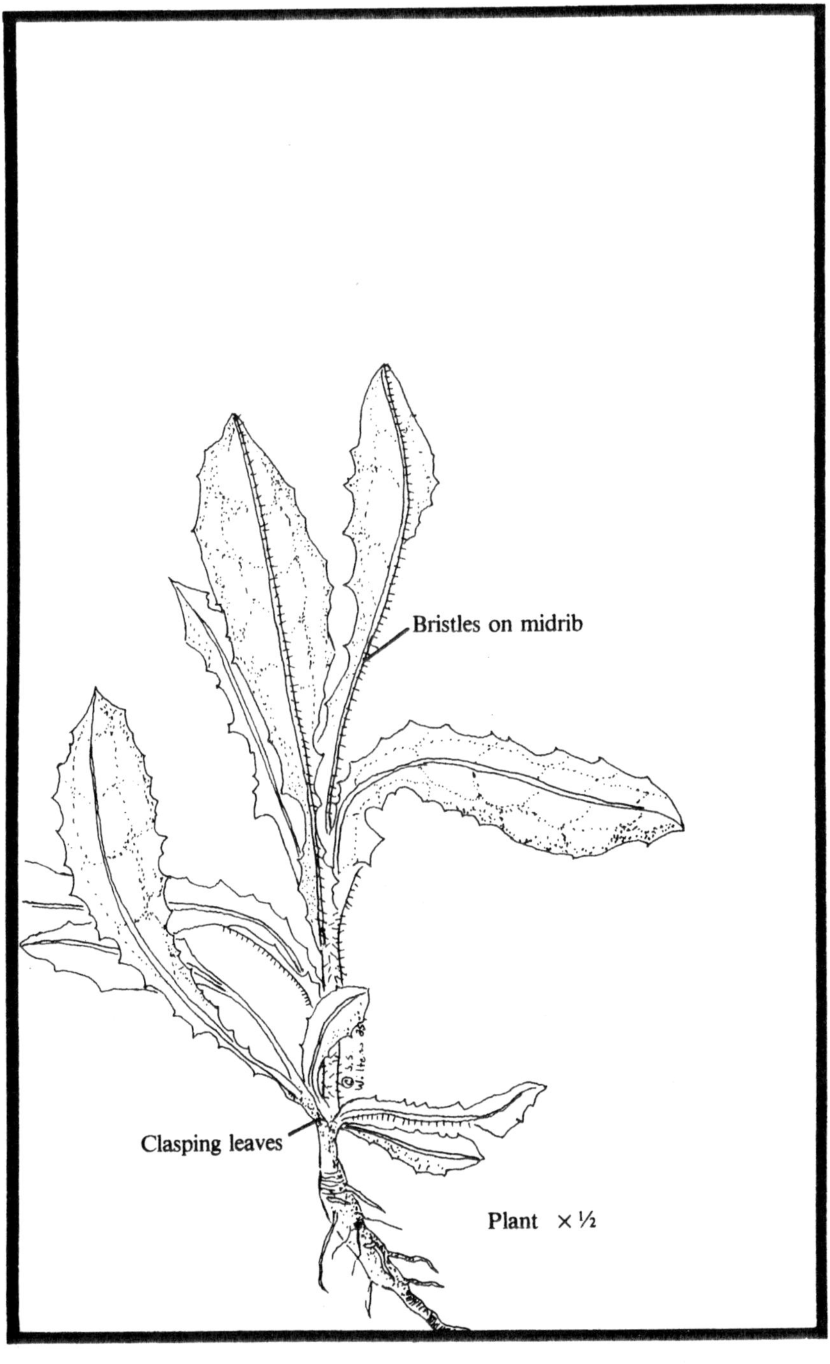

Prickly Lettuce (***Lactuca serriola***)

PRICKLY PEAR

Opuntia sps.
(Cactus Family: Cactaceae)

OTHER NAMES: Indian Fig, Beavertail Cactus

DESCRIPTION: This genus has a variety of species, many with common characteristics. Prickly Pears have large flat joints which are usually polka dotted with stiff noticeable spines, as well as less conspicuous miniature spines called glochids. It is interesting to note that the flattened pads are actually modified stems and the spines are highly modified leaves. The flowers are large showy blooms with a variety of colors, white to yellow to red. The fruits are door knob size, dotted with spines and a small crater depression in the top where the petals were originally attached.

HABITAT: Dry open hillsides, canyons, valleys, and as a hedgerow. Prefers dry sandy soil.

USES: Both the fruits (commonly referred to as tunas) and the thick fleshy pads (nopales) are edible. Fruits of the more common species in the Bay Area will ripen from green to a yellow or red color. Use a sharp long handled knife to sever the fruits from the pads into a bag. It's unwise to handle the fruit without gloves. Even though you may avoid the obvious spines, minute glochid bristles can become embedded in the skin, causing day-long irritation.

There are several methods for removing the spines from the fruit. One is to take a torch and singe the spines off. A slow pass of the torch is sufficient. If you are collecting a lot of fruit, it is easier to singe the spines while the fruit is still attached. If running around a cactus patch with a blow-torch affects your foraging sensitivity, then look forward to doing battle with the spiny fruits at home.

Another fruit cleaning technique that works nicely is to boil some water and, using tongs, plunge the tunas in for 1 minute. The spines become very flexible until they dry out again. When you have removed or softened the spines, slice the tuna lengthwise and, using a spoon, scoop out the seed-filled pulp.
The pulp may be eaten raw, seeds and all. The taste is similar to watermelon. I especially like the pulp in a drink called a cactus cooler:

CACTUS COOLER

1 cup cactus pulp
2 cups sparkling water
2 tbsps sugar

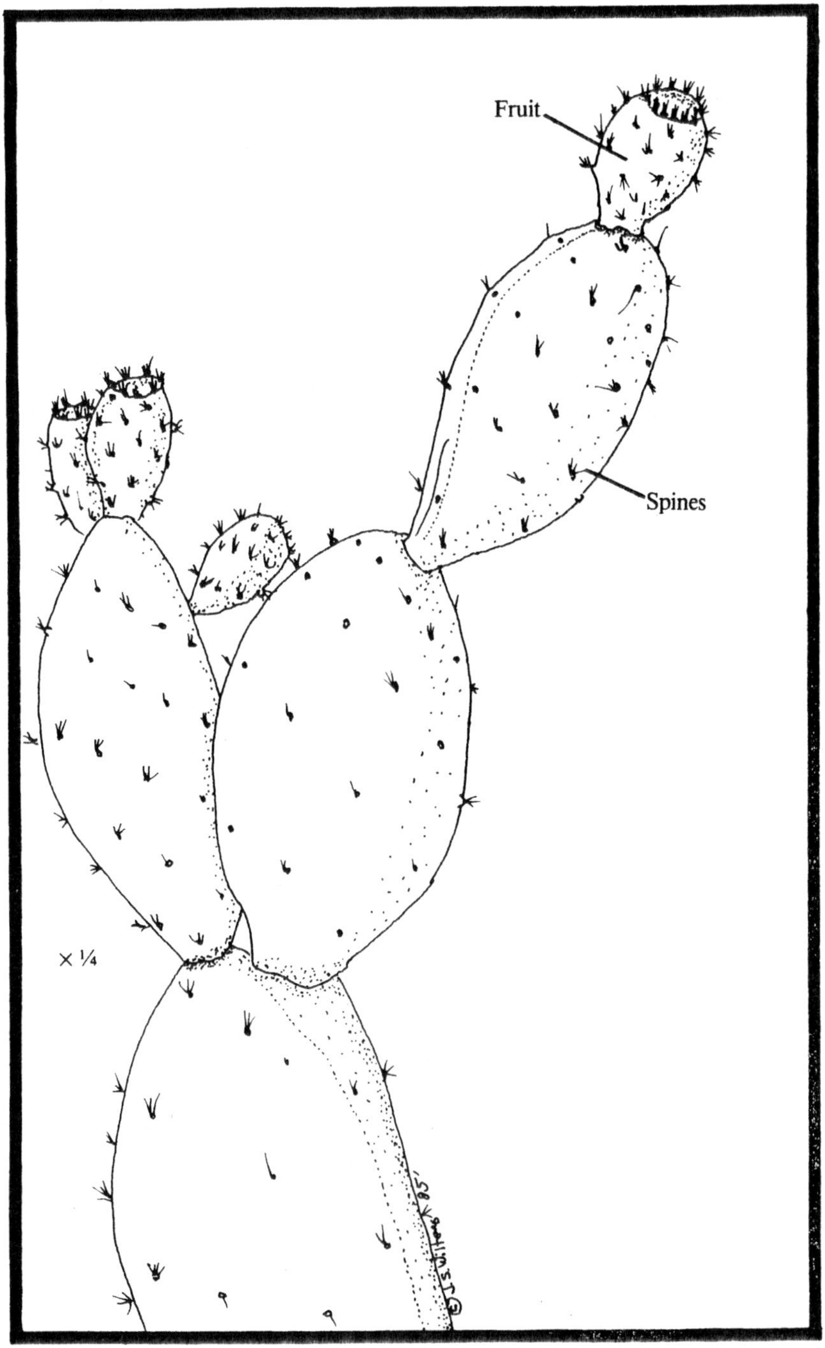

Prickly Pear (*Opuntia sp.*)

Pass the pulp through a metal mesh strainer to remove all the seeds. Add sugar to strained juice and then pour in sparkling water. Chill in a capped bottle and serve.

To use the pads as food, collect young spring pads 1 to 3 inches in diameter. Boil the pads for 20 minutes. Slice off the outer layer and trim the edges to remove the spines. It's wise to rinse your cutting board periodically to keep spines from collecting that will be passed to the cleaned pad. Rinse the cleaned pad under running water. The pads may be diced and added to salads and stews or used in a variety of dishes.

INTERESTING FACTS: The shiny green appearance of Prickly Pear pads is due to a thick wax layer. This wax layer retards water loss giving the plant a trump card to play in its desert environment.

Cactus pads were once boiled and the mucilaginous juice mixed with mortar to make it stick better to adobe houses.

Cactus is a native of the New World. It now has a world wide distribution. In 1787, cactus was introduced to Australia. Without any natural enemies to keep it in check, it spread over the continent and by 1925, 60,000,000 acres were adversely affected. The cactus was finally controlled by the introduction of a moth parasite that feeds on the cactus. This tiny moth quickly brought the cactus under control.

One species of Prickly Pear, *O. rufida*, is called Blind Prickly Pear. It lacks noticeable spines, but the tiny glochid bristles are still present. Cattle like to feed on the fruit and joints. If they are not careful, they may be blinded if glochids pierce the eyes.

PURSLANE

Portulaca oleracea
(Purslane Family: Portulacaceae)

OTHER NAMES: Pusley

DESCRIPTION: A prostrate fleshy herb. Stems somewhat reddish. Smooth leaves are paired and broadest near the apex. Yellow flowers in small clusters.

HABITAT: Open fields, vacant lots, common garden weed.

USES: Purslane has been used as a food plant since ancient times. The green plant may be used raw in salads or steamed for 5 minutes and served with butter. The seeds may be sprinkled on breads or puddings.

It is not necessary to pull up the whole plant, pinch off the stem and the plant will produce a new set of stems for later consumption. Make sure you wash the plant thoroughly as its close association with the ground often leaves it a bit gritty.

INTERESTING FACTS: Thoreau wrote of this plant in *Walden*, "I have made a satisfactory dinner on several accounts, simply off a dish of Purslane which I gathered in my cornfield, boiled and salted". He extended this observation by writing, "...yet men have come to such a pass that they frequently starve, not for want of necessities but for want of luxuries".

Purslane probably originated in India or China and is a recent import to the U.S. where it has become a well-established weed.

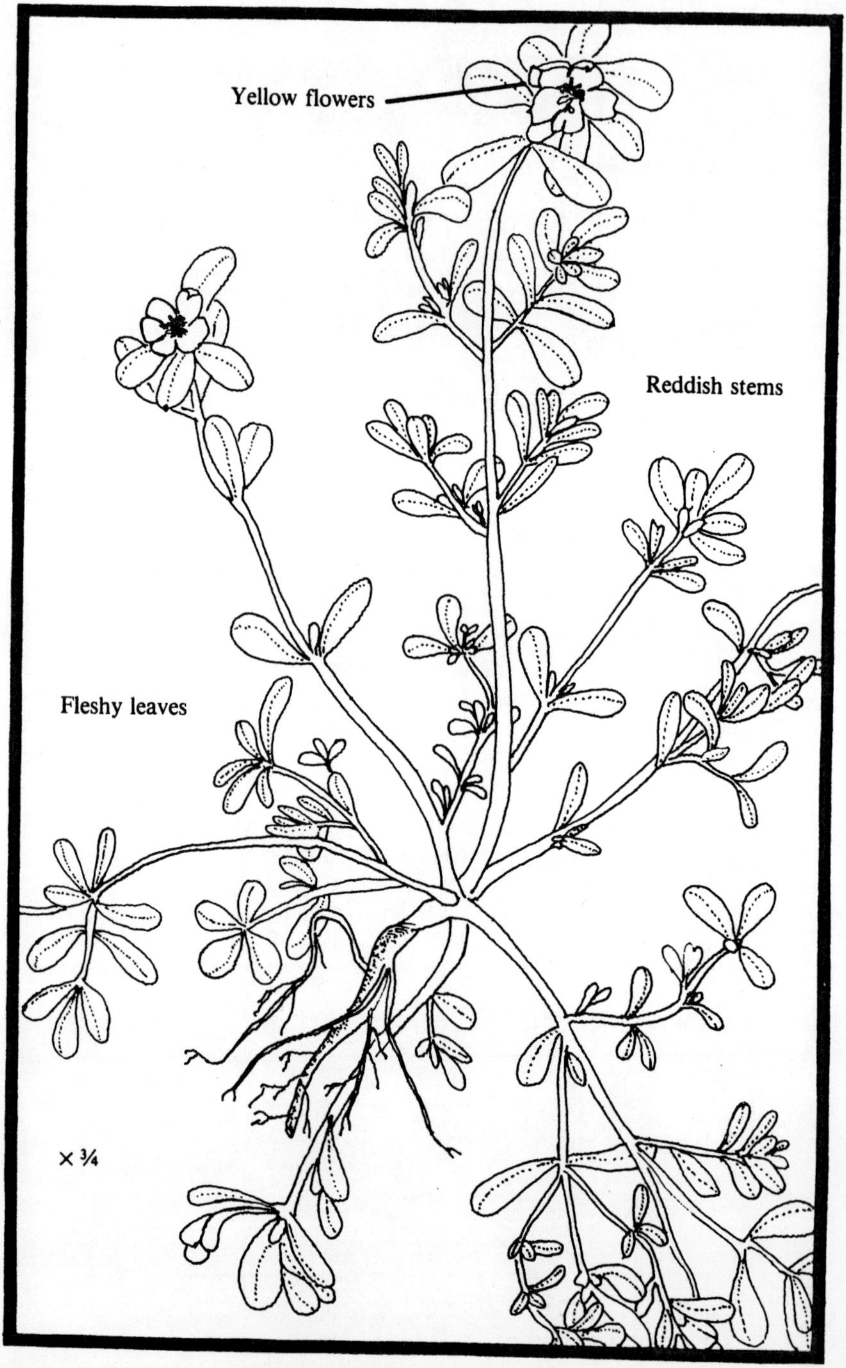

Purslane (*Portulaca oleracea*)

PYRACANTHA

Pyracantha coccinea
(Rose Family: Rosaceae)

OTHER NAMES: Firethorn

DESCRIPTION: Evergreen shrub. Glossy green leaves are narrow at base and widened at the tip, finely serrated margins. White flowers in compact clusters. Red berries hang in dense clusters. The berries will often remain on the plant for many months.

HABITAT: Common hedge planting, roadside landscaping, abandoned areas.

CAUTION: ***In England this species is implicated in the poisoning of children. The poisoning is supposedly due to cyanogenic glycosides. Fortunately, cooking removes the volatile cyanogens. It is interesting to note that apple seeds also contain cyanogenic glycosides and death has occurred as a result of eating a cupful of apple seeds.***

If you try the following recipe, make sure the Pyracantha bushes have not been sprayed with a pesticide.

USES: A jelly made from the cooked berries is quite appetizing. Collect ripe red berries and destem:

FIRETHORN JELLY

1 cup Pyracantha berries
½ cup water
½ cup sugar
1 tbsp lemon juice
pinch salt
1½ tbsp cornstarch

Simmer berries for 10 minutes in half a cup of salted water. Strain berries through a metal strainer pressing out all the juice. Add sugar and lemon juice. Dissolve cornstarch in half a cup of cold water in a separate container, then add to Pyracantha juice and simmer until thickened. Store in refrigerator.

INTERESTING FACTS: Many people with Pyracantha bushes in their yards as ornamental plants may recall seeing birds gorging themselves on the berries. These birds often display very un-bird like behavior, stumbling about, flying into walls and windows.

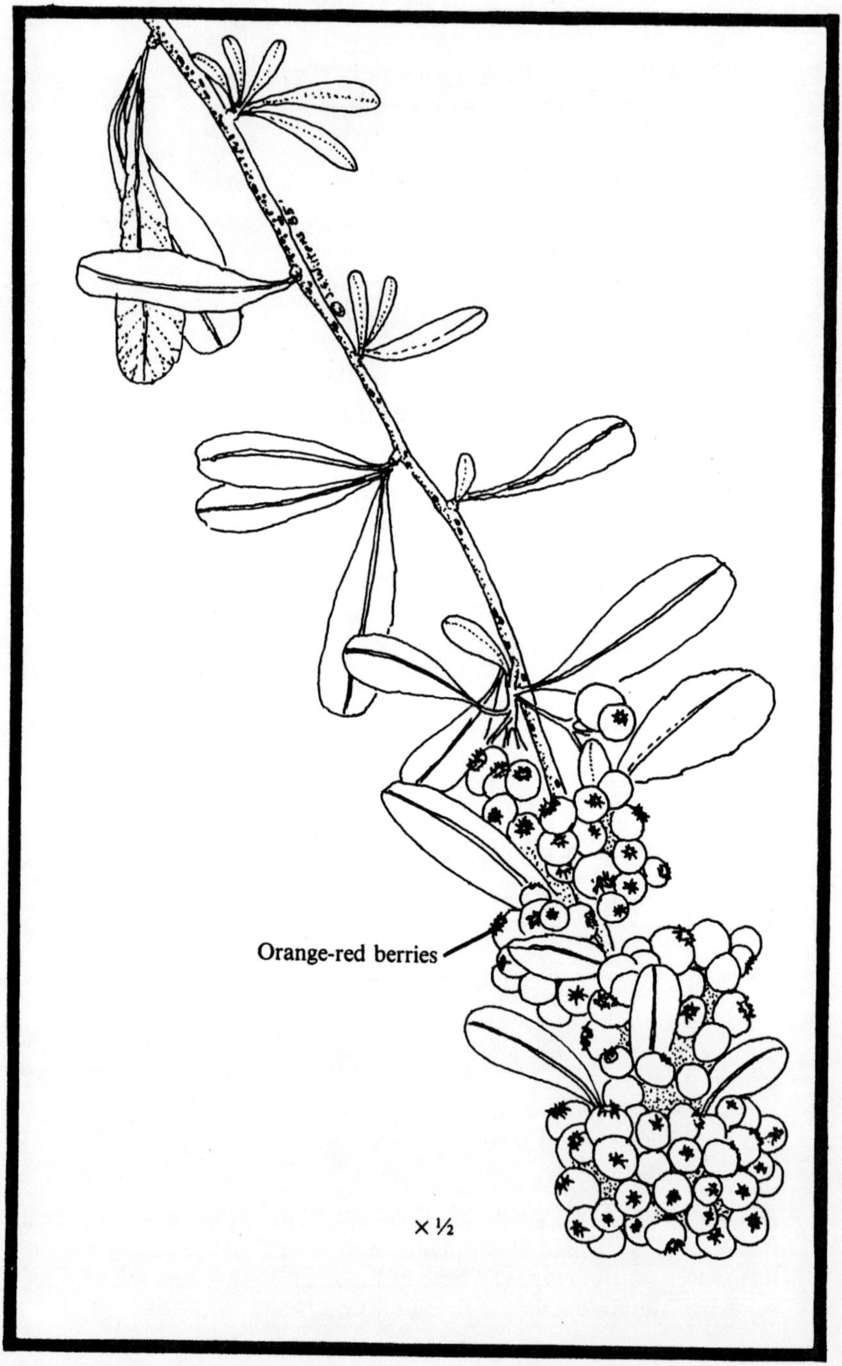

Pyracantha (*Pyracantha coccinea*)

In Santa Clara, just recently, the SPCA asked the highway department to remove Pyracantha bushes from along Hwy 101. When the berries are in a fermented state, they contribute to erratic bird behavior. Drunk birds would wobble out into the nearby roadway where they were hit by passing motorists. The birds weren't the only casualties, motorists trying to avoid the hundreds of birds (not to mention a number of cats attracted by easy prey) ended up creating a series of rear end collisions.

RADISH, WILD

Raphanus sativus
(Mustard Family: Cruciferae)

DESCRIPTION: An erect freely branching stem. Leaves are arranged alternately up the stem. Lower leaves are pinnately compound with the end section being rounded. Upper leaves are toothed along the outer margin. The 4 petaled flowers fade from reddish purple to white as the season progresses. Bluish venation may be seen in the white flowers. Seed pods are arranged alternately up the terminal portion of the stem. The pods are similar to mustard, but in Radish the base is swollen.

HABITAT: Hillsides, waste areas, vacant lots, recently plowed fields and orchards.

USES: The fresh leaves from young plants, prior to flowering, may be eaten raw in salads. Older leaves may be boiled as a spinach substitute. The flowers, before they open, have a pleasant Radish taste and may be added to salads or used as a garnish on other dishes. The seeds may also be eaten before they harden or made into a Radish spread (replace the mustard seeds for making mustard with Radish seeds).

The root of wild Radish tends to be fibrous as compared to its domesticated relatives.

INTERESTING FACTS: The Greeks valued the Radish so highly that when they made an offering to Apollo, they presented turnips in lead and beets in silver, whereas Radishes were presented in gold.

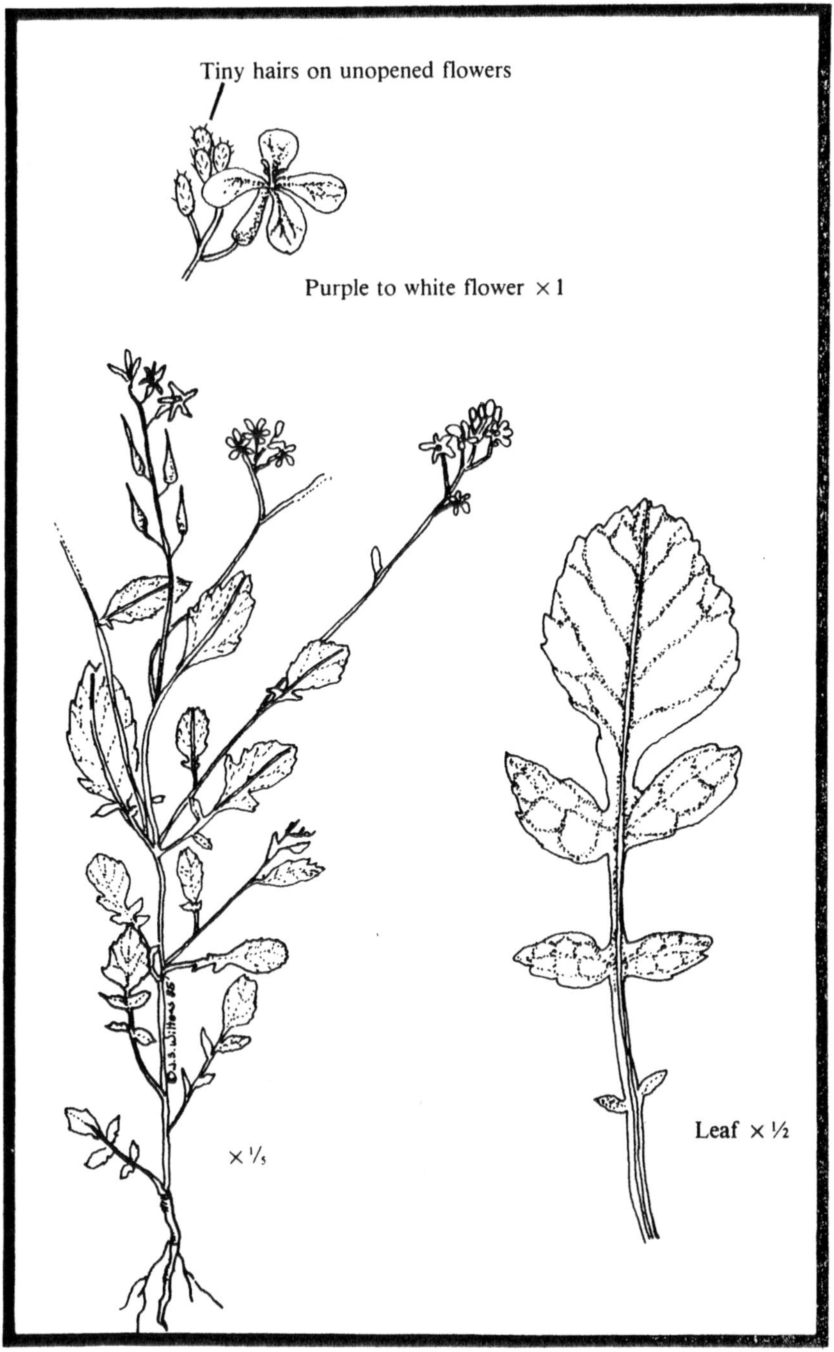

Radish, wild (*Raphanus sativus*)

ROSE, WILD

Rosa sps.
(Rose Family: Rosaceae)

DESCRIPTION: The different species of Roses have variable forms, from trailing vines, to shrubs to small trees. The stems of most species have sharp thorns. The pinnate leaves (refer to drawing) are ovate to elliptical with a finely serrated margin with a typical alternate arrangement up the stem. At the base of the leaves there are two stipules. Flower color is quite variable. Flowers usually have 5 petals and 5 sepals. The fruit is shaped like a small urn with the remains of the sepals forming a drooping star at the top.

HABITAT: Abandoned areas, fence rows, margin of creeks and woodlands.

CAUTION: *Avoid using Roses that have been treated with pesticides.*

USES: The fruit is referred to as a "hip". The hips are usually a bright red or orange and may be eaten raw after snipping off the remains of the withered flower and scrapping out the seeds. Dried hips can be stored and rehydrated at a later time for use in jams, jellies and pies.

Rose hip tea is made from the dried fruit. Steep about a quarter cup of the hips in hot water until they become soft. Crush the rehydrated fruits and wait serveral more minutes, then strain the liquid through cheesecloth. Add honey to taste.

The petals may be used to garnish dishes, though it's best to snip off the base of the petal as it has a somewhat bitter taste. The petals may also be used to make jam:

UNCOOKED ROSE PETAL JAM

1 cup Rose petals
¾ cup water
juice of a medium sized lemon
2½ cups sugar
1 package powdered pectin
¾ cup additional water

Remove petals and cut off bitter white tips. Pack petals into 1 cup and put in blender with ¾ cup water and lemon juice. Blend while adding sugar. Stir pectin in the additional ¾ cup water in a sauce pan and cook 1 minute stirring constantly. Pour this liquid into blender and blend with petal mixture.

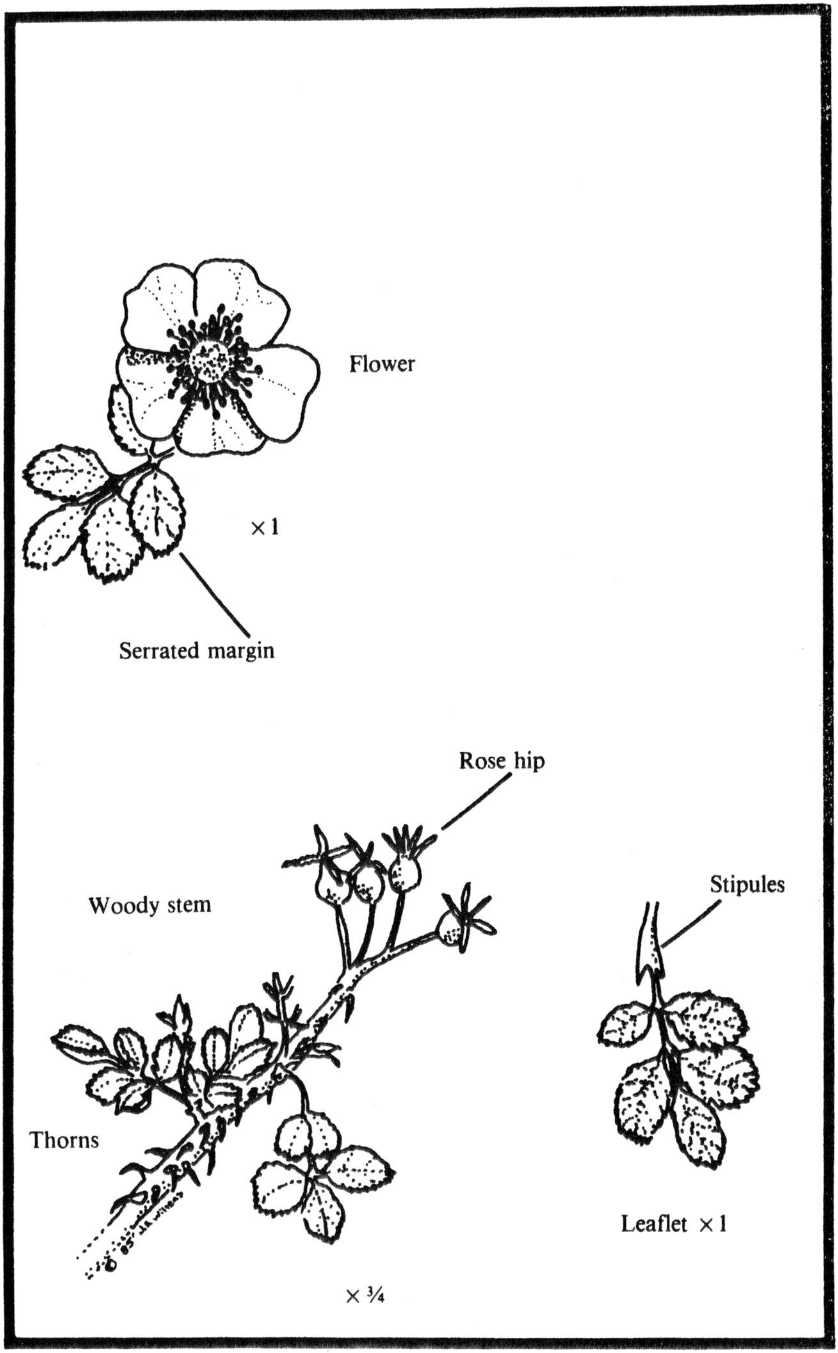

Rose, wild (*Rosa sp.*)

Pour mix into sterilized jars and store in the refrigerator. Storage time is about 1 month. If you want it to last longer, then freeze some.

INTERESTING FACTS: The vitamin C content of Rose hips has been shown to be 60 times higher than that of lemons. During WW II, when there were not enough oranges, a number of European countries collected rose hips and processed them into a syrup rich in vitamin C.

In an emergency, fishing hooks can be made from the thorns.

Rose water, famed for its fragrance, can be made by placing a handful of rose petals in a tightly sealed jar containing a cup of water.

ROSEMARY

Rosmarinus officinalis
(Mint Family: Labiatae)

DESCRIPTION: A shrubby plant, two to six feet tall. Narrow leaves are dark green above and grayish beneath. Small lavender-blue flowers. The plant is distinctly aromatic.

HABITAT: Common garden ornamental, divider strips, dry foothill areas.

USES: Rosemary is used as a seasoning for soups and stews.

INTERESTING FACTS: This fragrant herb has found a variety of uses other than culinary. A tea can be made to freshen the breath. Sachets of the herb have been sewn into pillows to make for a fragrant night's sleep. It has also been mixed in with tobacco for taste considerations. And sprigs of the plant suspended in your closet are thought to be beneficial in repelling moths.

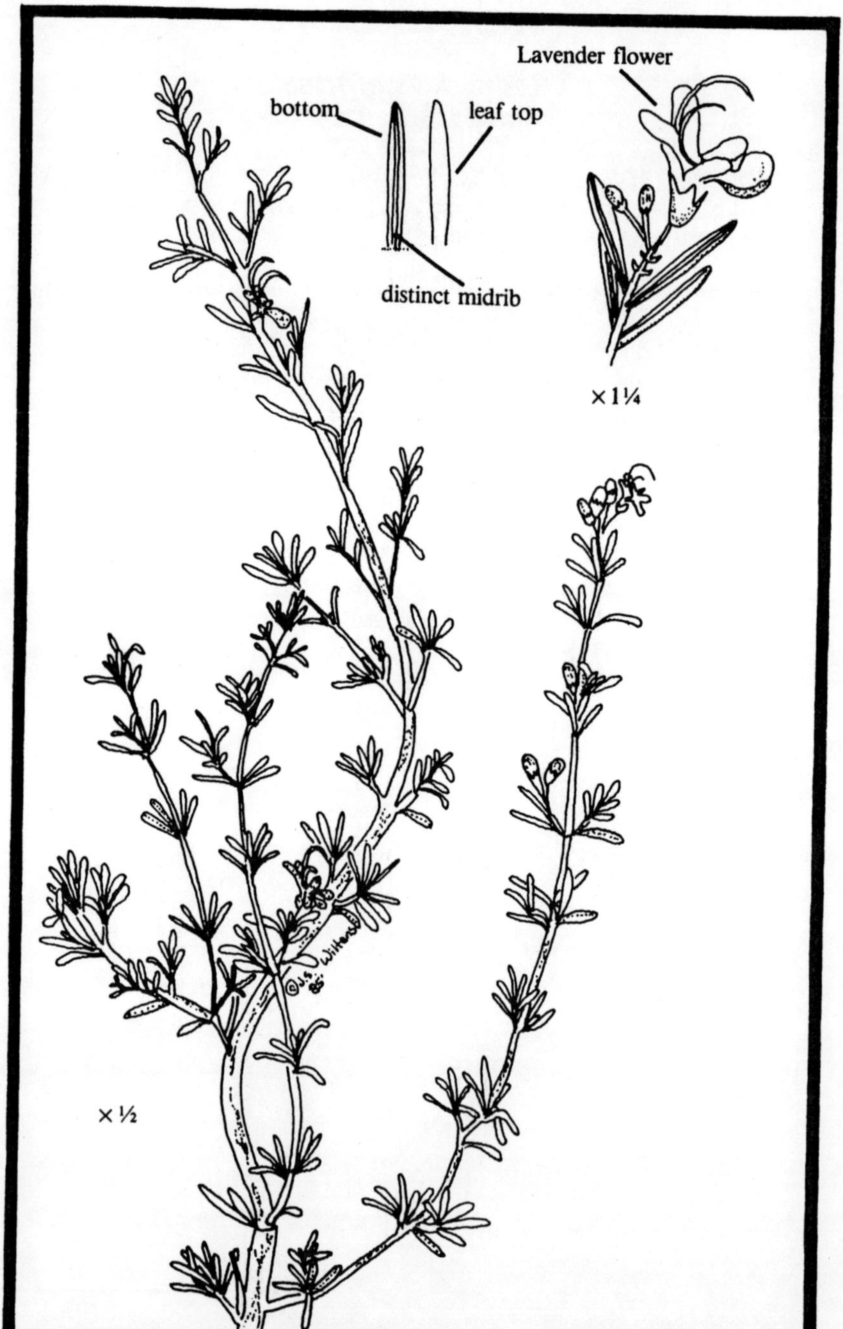

Rosemary (*Rosmarinus officinalis*)

SHEPHERD'S PURSE

Capsella bursa-pastoris
(Mustard Family: Cruciferae)

OTHER NAMES: Lady's Slipper, Pepper and Salt, Mothers Heart

DESCRIPTION: An upright stalk, which may or may not be branched, arises from a basal rosette of leaves. Basal leaves are deeply incised with the terminal portion of the leaf being the largest. The stem bears a few clasping leaves with toothed margins. Small white flowers are borne in a terminal cluster at the end of the upright stalk. The most noticeable feature is the flat, heart-shaped seed pods borne along the upright stem. Seeds are orange-brown.

HABITAT: Waste places, vacant lots, fields, open areas.

USES: Collect the basal rosette of leaves before flowering. Steam leaves for 5 minutes, then serve with butter. If you find the leaves are a little too peppery for your taste, place a sheet of canvas over the leaves for several days prior to picking. This will slightly blanch the leaves and make them milder.

The heart shape seed pods may be stripped from the plant by running your hand up the length of the stem. Though the Indians are supposed to have winnowed the seeds for making a flat bread, I find the process is too tedious for the less patient modern man. I prefer to use the green pods whole, either in a garnish on salads, in an omelet or as a substitute for pepper.

The thin root can be pulled from the ground, if the soil is moist, and used as a ginger substitute.

INTERESTING FACTS: Shepherd's Purse is not native to North America, but is an Old World import.

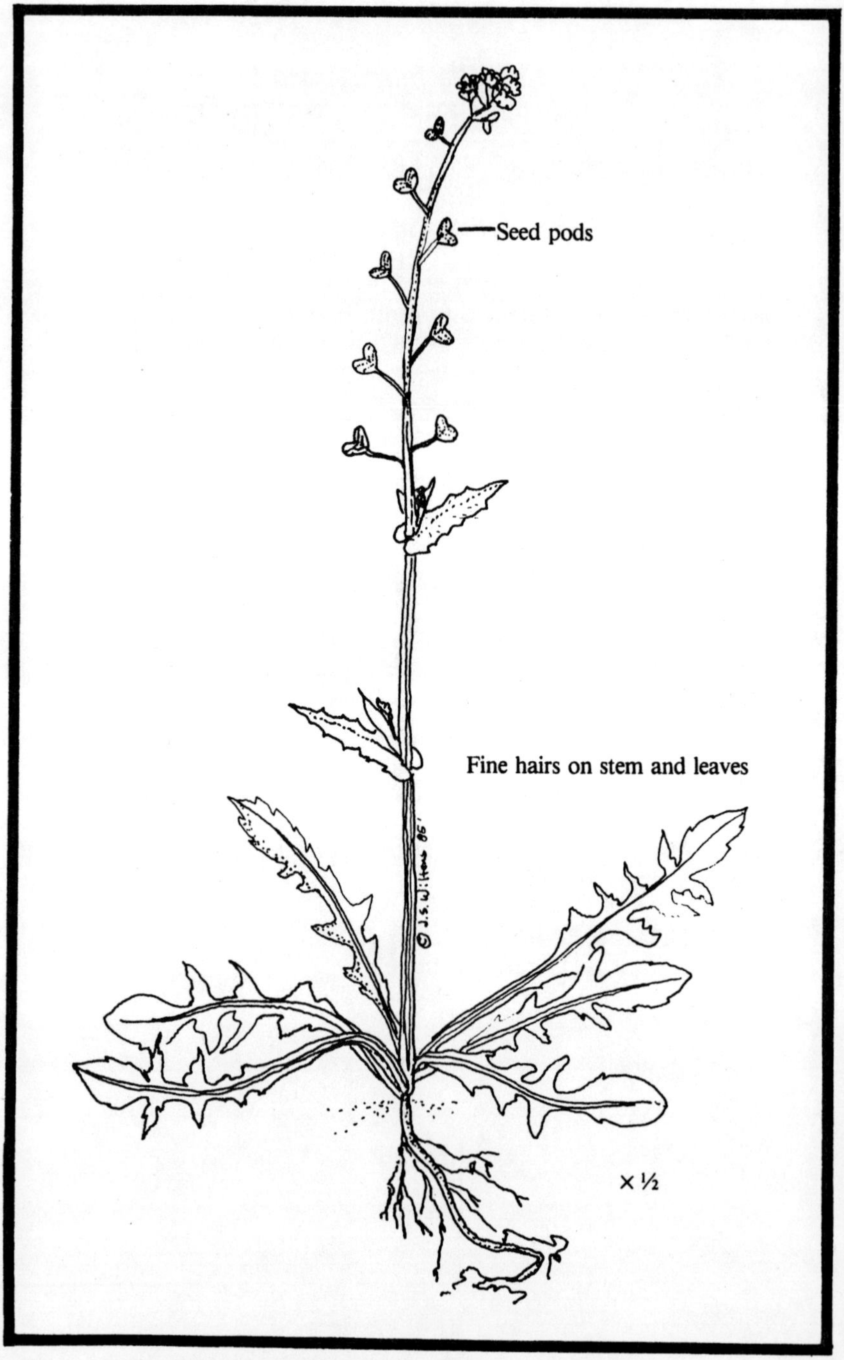

Shepherd's Purse (*Capsella bursa–pastoris*)

SOW THISTLE

Sonchus oleraceus
(Sunflower Family: Compositae)

OTHER NAMES: Milk Thistle

DESCRIPTION: Annual. Young plants are similar to dandelion, but leaves originate in an ascending pattern along a stem that elongates with age. Deeply lobed leaves have a distinct triangular outline on mature tips. In older plants the leaves clasp the stem. Look along the leaf margin for soft tiny spines. Broken leaves exude a milky sap. Leaves are green on top, whitish on bottom. Stems often have a purple discoloration. Yellow composite (dandelion like) flowers, borne on stems in axils of the leaves. The seeds are set in a fluffy head. Seeds are attached directly to their parachute tufts in distinction to dandelions which have a thin filament separating the seed from its parachute.

USES: Very young leaves can be used in salads. Leaves become increasingly bitter with age and require boiling for 3-5 minutes.

INTERESTING FACTS: The whitish sap that oozes from cut parts of the plant has been processed into an agent to fight opium addiction.

The common name, Sow Thistle, comes from the fact that pigs eagerly consume the plant.

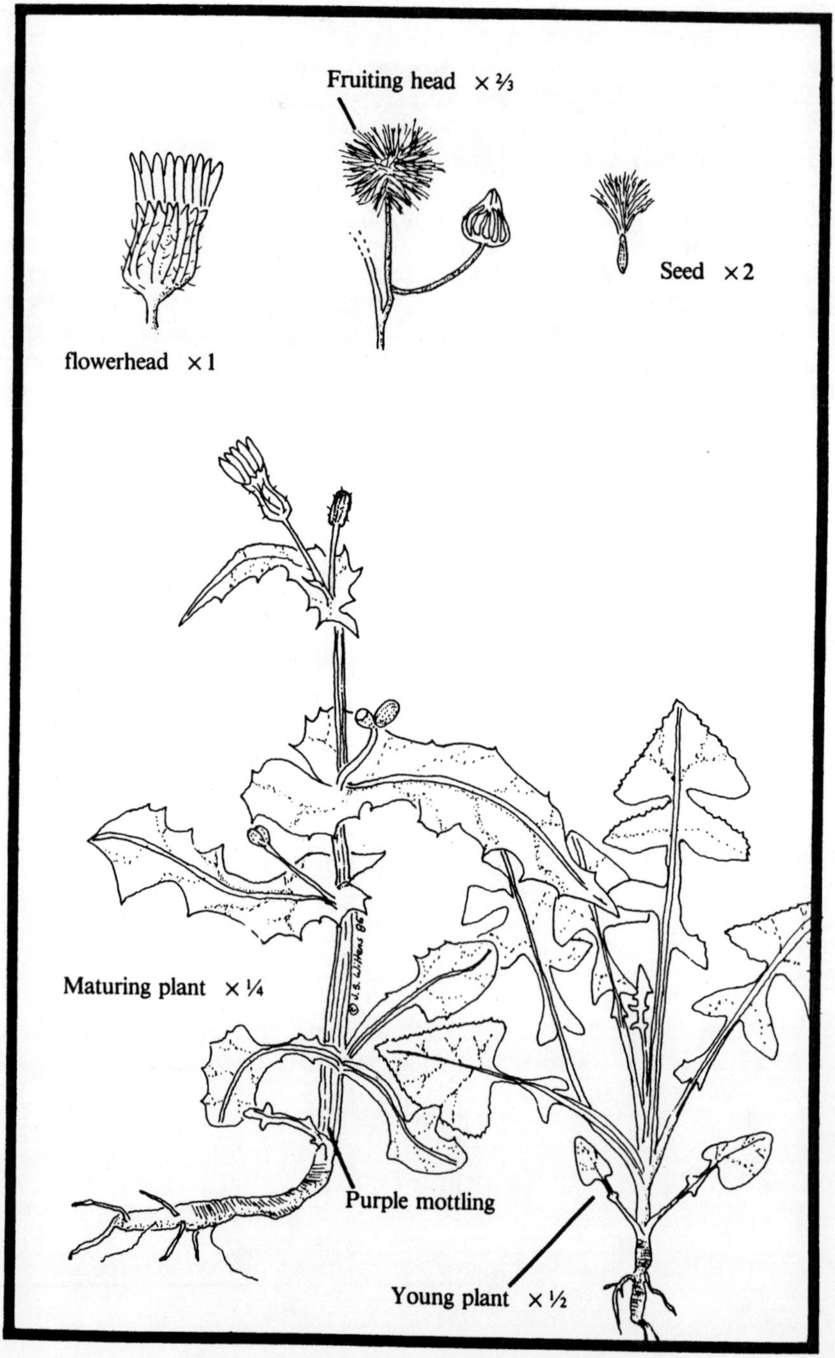

Sow Thistle (*Sonchus oleraceus*)

SPEARMINT

Mentha spicata
(Mint Family: Labiatae)

DESCRIPTION: The erect stems arise from a creeping rootstalk. The stem has four distinct sides, a boxed tube. The leaves are opposite one another on very short or non-existent petioles (leaf stems). The leaves are arranged on the stems in a spiral fashion. The leaf has an oblong to lance shape with a serrated margin. Small purple flowers occur in tight clusters at a portion of the end of the stem.

HABITAT: Moist areas, margin of streams.

USES: I have found quite a variation in the taste of Spearmint, probably dependent on growing conditions. Try and find a patch that you are partial to; some beds fall short of what we expect Spearmint to taste like. Collect leaves at any stage of growth.

To make tea, pour a cup of boiling water over ½ cup of fresh leaves, steep for about 10 minutes (do not boil the leaves as this volatizes the aromatic oils).

Spearmint can also be used to make jams and jellies and for seasoning in a variety of recipes.

Try adding fresh Spearmint leaves to your next oil-and-vinegar salad. Chop a half cup of leaves into fine pieces and mix in salad.

INTERESTING FACTS: Spearmint can easily be transplanted to your yard by pulling up an underground stem, trimming back the leaves and planting in a moist area. The biggest problem is keeping the Spearmint contained, as it has a tendency to spread.

Look carefully at the arrangement of leaves along a Spearmint stem. You will note that there is a distinct spiral pattern. This serves an important function. The spiral pattern results in leaves getting as little shading from adjacent leaves as possible. This helps to ensure efficient photosynthesis (use of sunlight to manufacture plant food).

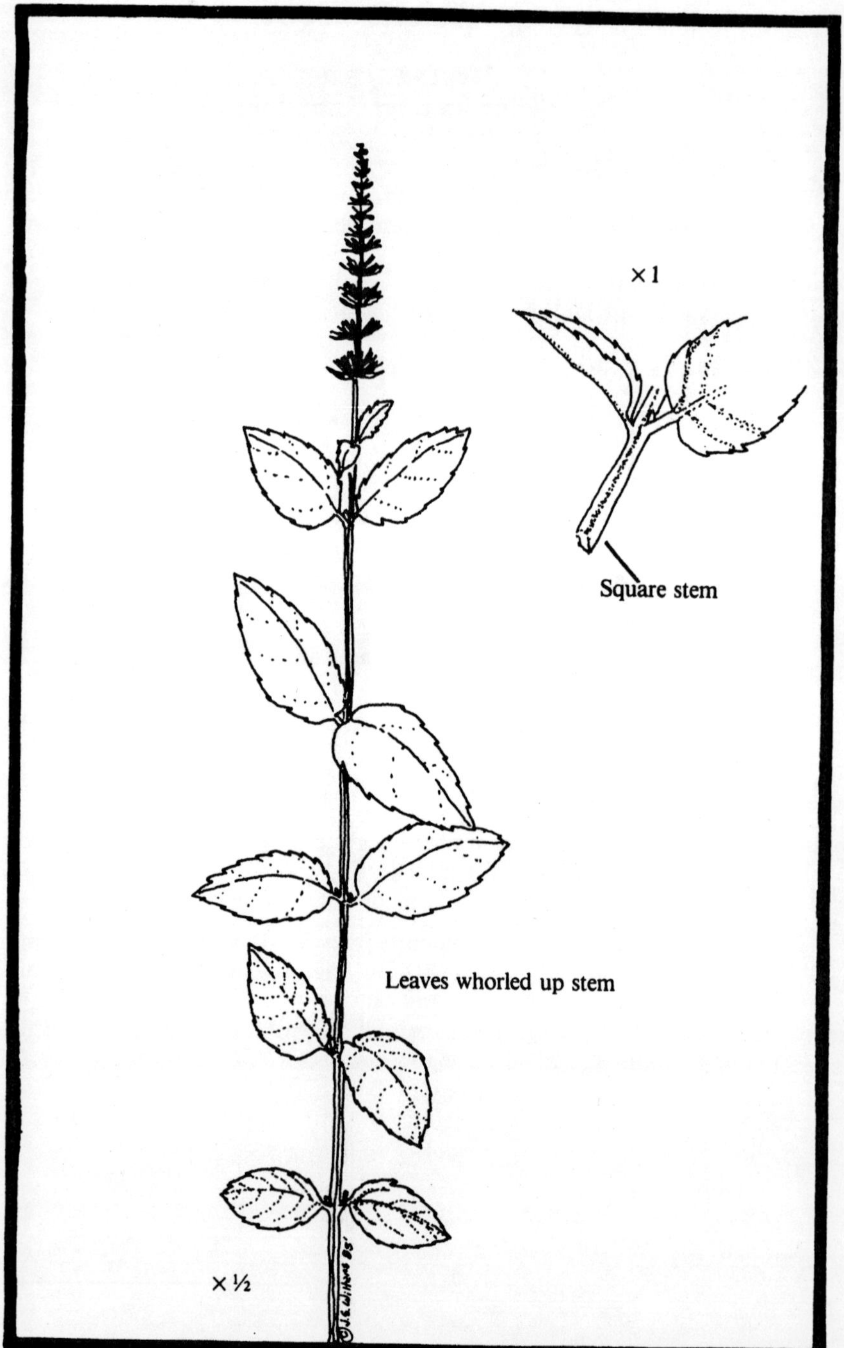

Spearmint (*Mentha spicata*)

STINGING NETTLE

Urtica holosericea
(Nettle Family: Urticaceae)

DESCRIPTION: Stout usually unbranched 4-sided stems arise from an underground rootstalk. Leaves are opposite one another on the stem and have a broad lanceolate shape, prominent veins and a coarsely serrated margin. Stems and bottom of leaves are covered by a fine fuzz as well as tiny visible stinging spines. Tiny green flowers in hanging racemes arise from the leaf axils.

HABITAT: Moist areas, stream banks, margins of woods and trails. Prefers diffuse sunlight.

CAUTION: ***The plant is covered by fine stinging hairs. Each hair is hollow with a bulbous base that contains potent irritants: acetycholine, histamine and serotinin. When you contact the plant, the tiny hollow hairs penetrate the skin and the bulb injects the poison. The intense burning subsides rapidly but a nagging irritation may last 24-48 hours.*** Brush up against this plant and you will discover how it got its common name. As child I have a vivid memory of reaching for a handhold and grabbing a Stinging Nettle. The response was no less dramatic than sticking my finger in a 120 volt socket. As I tumbled head-over-heels backwards into a creek bed, I made it a point to never forget this particular plant.

USES: It never ceases to amaze me that such a hostile plant can be eaten with proper preparation. Collect the very young plants when they are no more than several inches high. If you collect older plants, even with proper preparation, they will have a gritty taste. This is due to the presence of cystoliths, calcium carbonate granules, that form as the plant matures. When collecting the plant, make sure you avoid the stinging hairs by wearing thick gloves or snipping the plants directly into a bag.

The easiest way to prepare Nettle is to simply boil it for 10 to 20 minutes and serve with a little butter. The stinging property is removed by boiling. The water left over from boiling can be mixed with a little honey to make a tea. If you like the green tea they commonly serve in Chinese restaurants you have a foretaste of what Nettle tea is like.

Nettle can be used to make a rennet as it coagulates milk. To make a Nettle junket, heat one pint of milk to lukewarm, stir in 2 tablespoons of sugar, ½ teaspoon almond extract, and 1 teaspoon of Nettle juice (obtained by boiling) to which a ½ teaspoon of salt has been added. Pour into glasses and refrigerate.

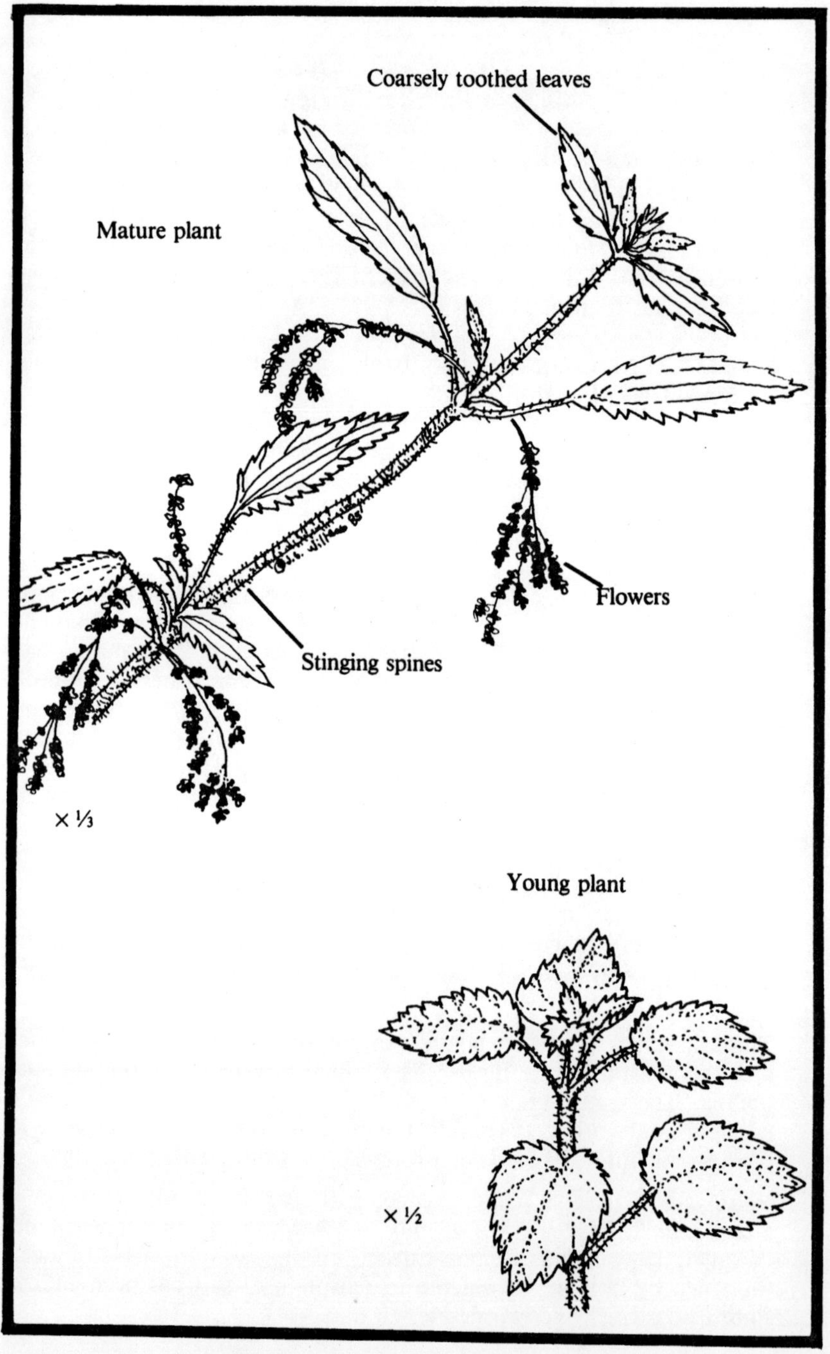

Stinging Nettle (*Urtica holosericea*)

INTERESTING FACTS: Nettle is high in vitamins C and A and is a rich source of protein.

Many healing properties have been attributed to this plant. One of which is a treatment for rheumatism, which involves rubbing the fresh plant over the affected part. The question in this case would be, which is better, the cure or the affliction.

Nettle has often been used as a source for fiber. The main stalk is dried, then lightly pounded in a stream to remove the vegetable material, leaving behind the fiber which can be woven into cord, clothing and baskets.

Nettle has been shown to be a valuable forage food. Animals won't touch the plant in its fresh state, but after drying, which destroys the stinging principle, it is an eagerly sought-after plant.

The Cahuilla Indians of California would occasionally whip disobedient children with Nettle, an uncommon event since children were rarely punished.

Roman soliders were also known to use the plant in self-inficted flagellation prior to going into battle. Supposedly this practice would incite the soliders and make them more insensitive to pain they might encounter on the battlefield.

STORKSBILL

Erodium cicutarium and moschatum
(Geranium Family: Geraniaceae)

OTHER NAMES: Filaree, Scissors Plant, Clocks

DESCRIPTION: Leaves arise from a basal rosette. Leaves are pinnately compound (arranged on each side of a common axis), deeply cleft with a serrated margin. Fine hairs cover leaf stem, top of leaf and veins on leaf bottom (be certain that hairs cover the plant so you don't confuse it with Poison Hemlock '*Conium maculatum*', which is hairless). The 5 petaled flowers are rose to violet. Seeds are housed in an awl shaped structure. When the seeds are released they are attached to a corkscrew shaped filament.

HABITAT: Common weed in waste areas, vacant lots, fields and roadsides.

USES: The fresh stems and leaves of young plants can be used raw in salads or boiled and served like spinach. Can also be added to vegetable soups. An excellent spinach substitute.

INTERESTING FACTS: The genus name is derived from the Greek word "erodios", which means heron, an obvious reference to the similarities of the seed capsule with a heron's bill.

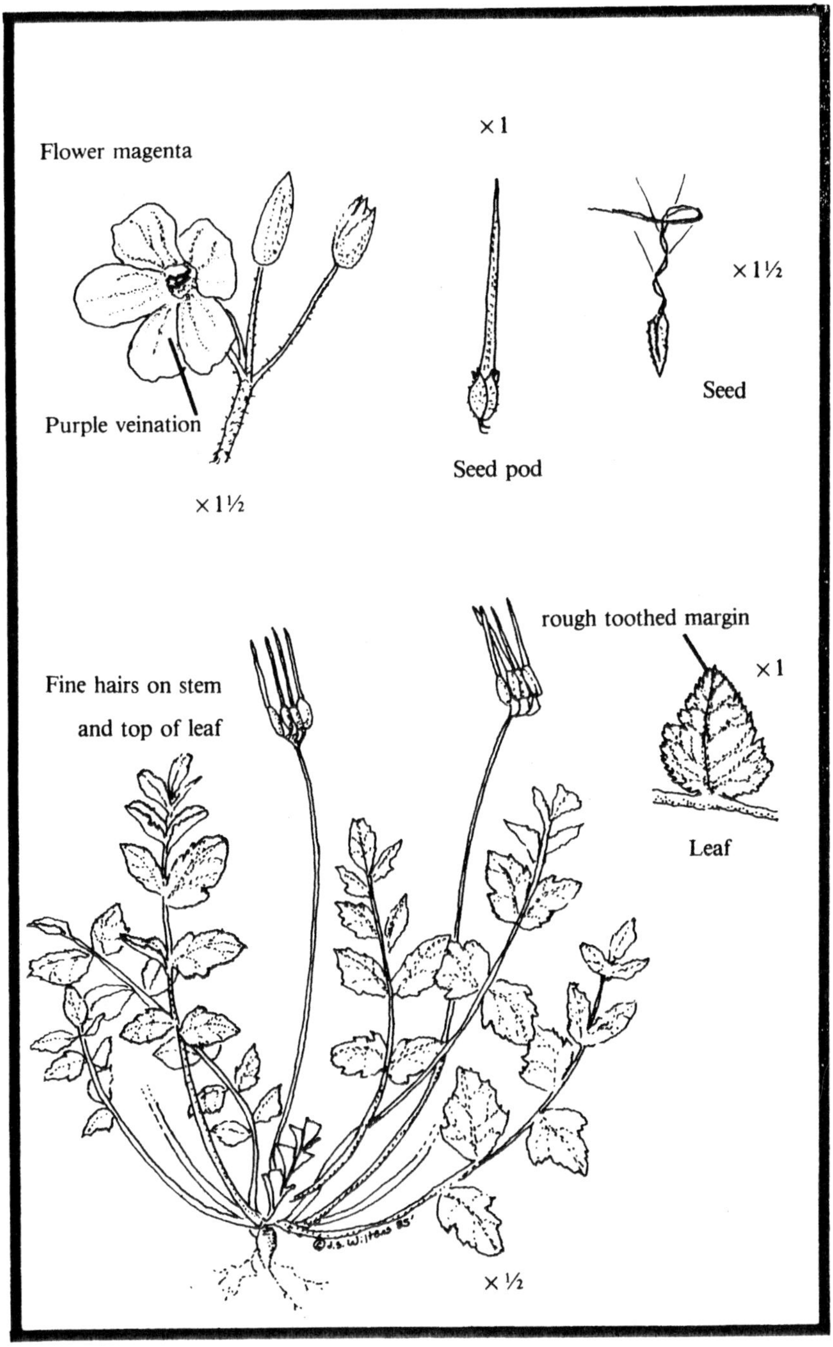

Storksbill (*Erodium cicutarium*)

STRAWBERRY, WILD

Fragaria vesca **subspecies** ***californica***
formerly ***F. californica***
(Rose Family: Rosaceae)

OTHER NAMES: Wood Strawberry

DESCRIPTION: Leaves are borne on elongate petioles originating from a short rootstock. Leaflets in groups of 3 with a coarsely serrated margin. The petioles and leaves are covered with fine silky hairs. Five petaled white flowers. Fruits are similar to their supermarket brethren only smaller.

HABITAT: Open woodlands, margins of woodlands and fields.

USES: Raw, dried, cooked, jammed, just about any way you can.

STRAWBERRY FRUIT LEATHER

1 cup Strawberries
½ tbsp honey

Mash berries thoroughly. Add honey. Place in a sauce pan and just bring to a boil. Pour thin layer (a stack of 3 pennies is the right thickness) onto a teflon cookie sheet. Set the oven to its lowest setting and dry the Strawberry puree for 6-7 hours. When the strawberries have reached a leathery consistency, roll and seal in Saran Wrap.

To make Strawberry tea, take two handfuls of green leaves and immerse in 1 qt. boiling water for 5 minutes.

INTERESTING FACTS: The Strawberry can reproduce by means of vegetative runners that spread along the ground. These runners may be the reason we call this plant the Strawberry. Because the runners appeared to be strewn over the ground, and the ancient word for strewed was 'strawed', the plant was called 'strawedberry' which was eventually shortened to Strawberry.

Strawberries are a rich source of vitamins A and C.

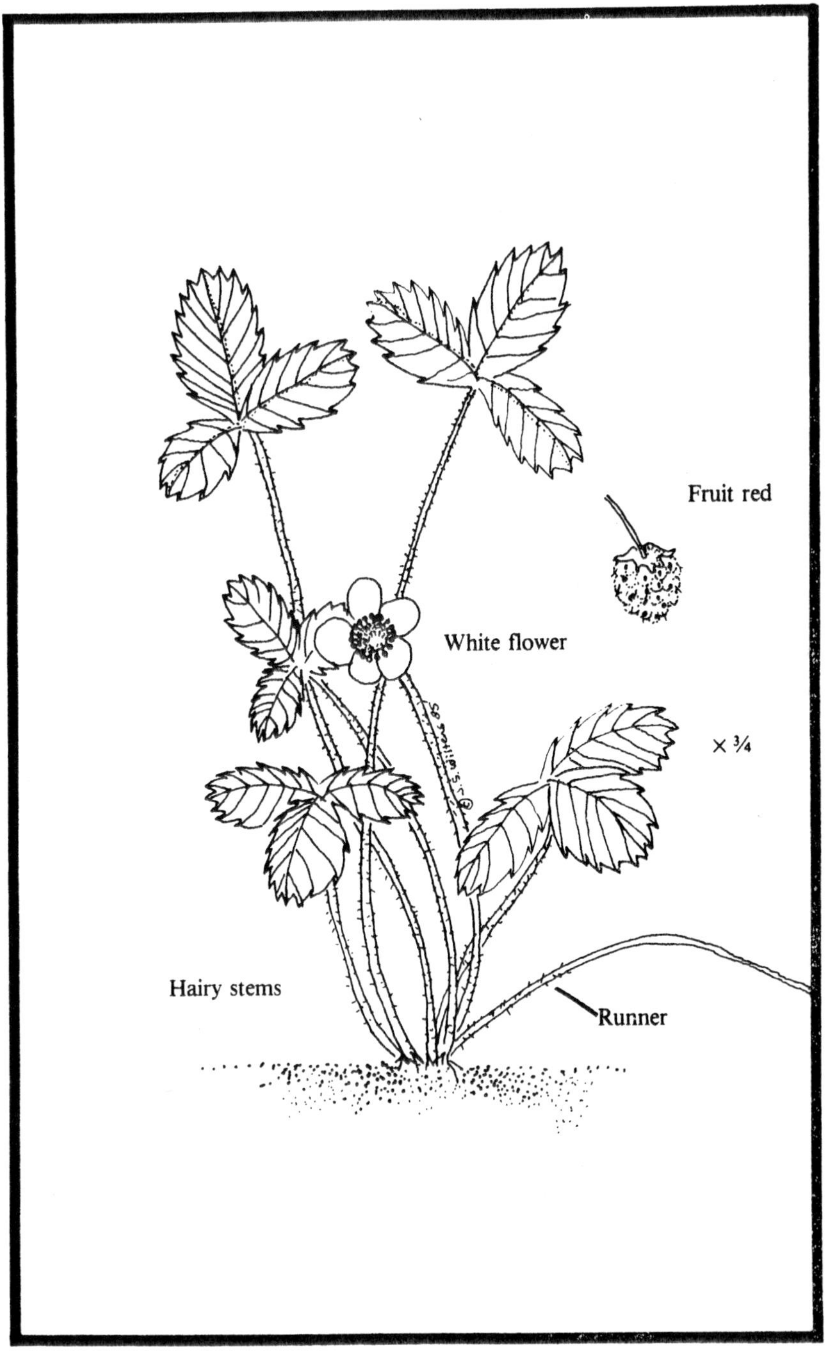

Strawberry (*Fragaria vesca*)

THISTLE

Cirsium vulgare
(Sunflower Family: Compositae)

OTHER NAMES: Bull Thistle, Bur Thistle, Common Thistle.

DESCRIPTION: The spindly upright Thistle is 2-5 feet high. The elongate deeply indented leaves are tipped with painfully sharp prickles. The leaves alternate up the stem. Flowers originate from egg shaped burr-like structures. The bright purple-red bristles of the flower are quite noticeable.

HABITAT: Fields, meadows, vacant lots, disturbed areas.

USES: The stem of the young Thistle (prior to flowering) may be peeled of its fibrous outer layer and cooked as greens.

Thistle roots may be eaten boiled or roasted, but they have a rather bland taste.

The Thistle is related to the artichoke. If you find a stand of Thistles with particularly large flower heads (but prior to actual flowering) remove the heads and boil like artichokes and eat in the same manner. The amount of "meat" at the base of the leaf is meager but tasty.

INTERESTING FACTS: In the late 1800's, while exploring Yellowstone, Truman Everts became separated from the main group. Not only was he lost, but he also managed to lose his glasses upon which he depended heavily. It was over a month before he was found. During this time he survived by eating Thistles.

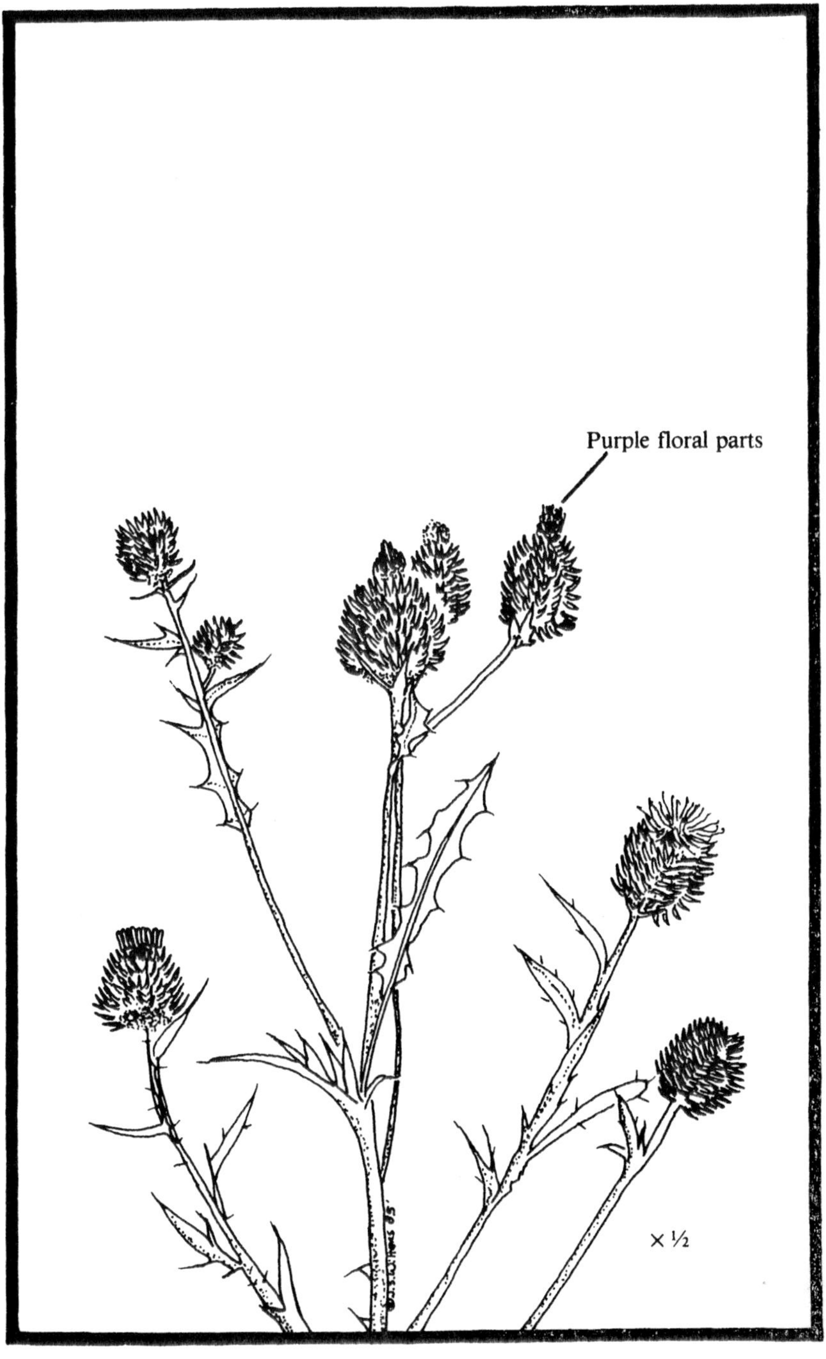

Thistle (*Cirsium sp.*)

WATERCRESS

Nasturtium officinale
(Mustard Family: Cruciferae)

OTHER NAMES: Pepper Leaf

DESCRIPTION: Pick up a stem of Watercress and break it open. You will notice that it is hollow inside, this provides flotation for this predominantly aquatic plant. The leaves are mostly pinnate with 3-11 smooth shiny green leaflets in an alternate arrangement on each branch. White roots originate at the leaf nodes and anchor the plant. Flowers are white. When the plant is crushed, it has a subtle peppery odor. Older parts are red veined.

HABITAT: Found in slow moving streams, either prostrate on the water or growing a short distance up the bank where it may form dense mats.

CAUTION: ***Since this plant often grows in close proximity to Poison Hemlock (Conium maculatum), you should know the obvious differences between the two.*** In March 1976, two men camping in the Santa Cruz mountains, mistook Poison Hemlock for Watercress. One man died, the other managed to get out and get help. Watercress really has very little resemblance to Poison Hemlock, but, for the untrained, gross errors can be made.

Pick Watercress from unpolluted streams. For many years, my source was a spring bubbling from the ground on my parents' ranch. Since the water was periodically tested for contamination, I felt reasonably safe about the Watercress.

But, you can't be too careful. If you are unsure about the water then soak the Watercress in water containing iodine purification tablets (one brand name is Aqua Pure).

Chlorine tablets are often recommended in some books, but chlorine tablets are of dubious value. The excess organic material provided by the Watercress has a tendency to neutralize the fast acting chlorine disinfectants, not leaving sufficient residual for bacterial, protozoal and viral substances.

If you are really skeptical about the water, boiling or steaming the Watercress is probably the most effective preventive.

USES: Twist young sprigs from the main stem. There's no reason to destroy the whole plant. It will put out new growth from the main stem, and you don't want the stem anyway. It is too fibrous.

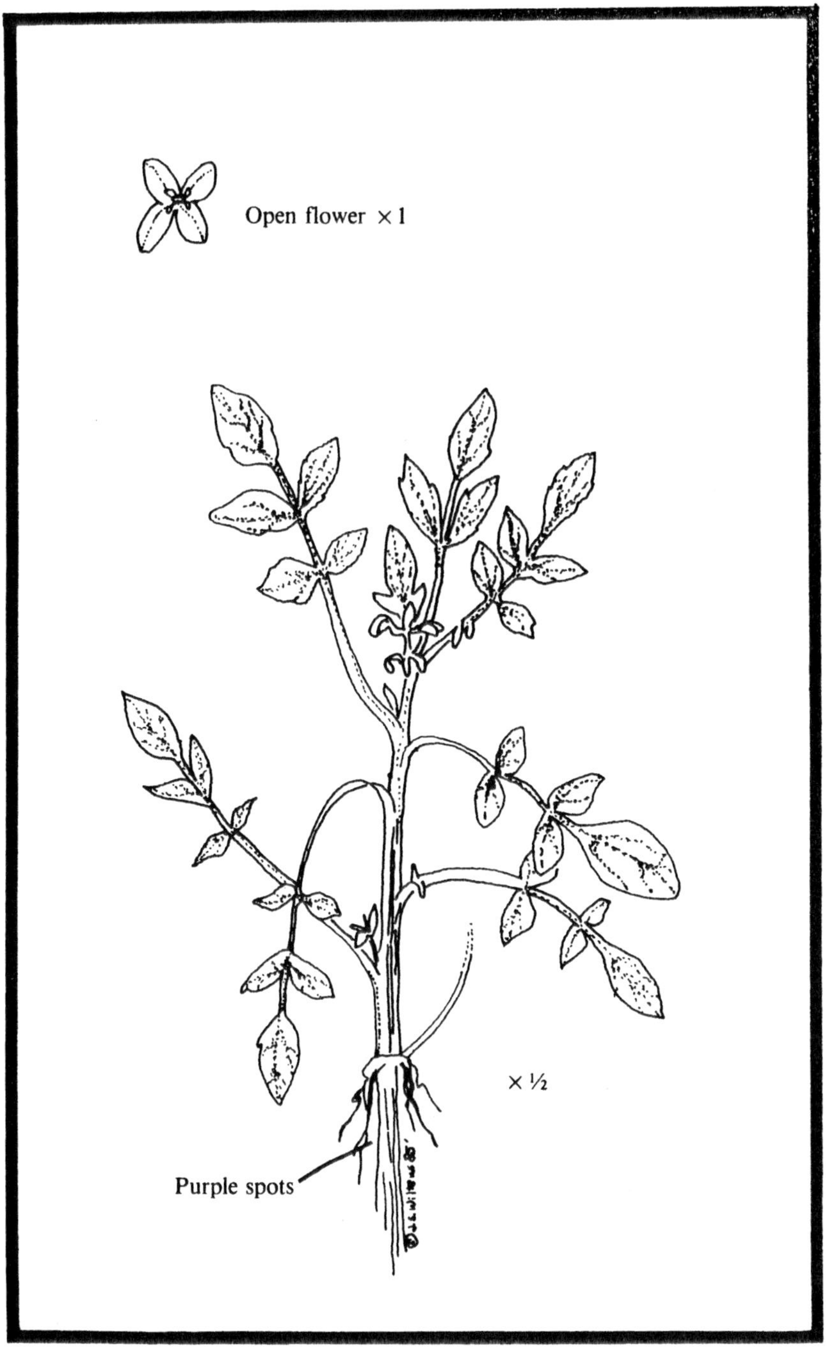

Watercress (*Nasturtium officinale*)

Fresh Watercress can be used to spice up a salad or used as the classic garnish on sandwiches or main dishes. Watercress may also be boiled and used similar to spinach.

An oriental approach to Watercress is especially appetizing:

WOK'D WATERCRESS

½ lb. Watercress
2 tbsps cooking oil
2 tbsps soy sauce

Heat the cooking oil in a wok, add Watercress and stir for 4 minutes or until Watercress wilts. Remove from the burner and toss with soy sauce. Serve while still hot.

INTERESTING FACTS: Watercress ranks high in vitamins C, A, B and E.

Watercress is a hardy little plant and can reproduce by seed or vegetative reproduction. If you look carefully at the junction to the branches you will notice tiny rootlets. If the main stem is broken and the pieces tossed in a stream, there is a good chance that the plant will lodge along the bank and the roots will grow out and re-attach the plant.

POISONOUS PLANTS

Some poisonous plants of Northern California

BUCKEYE, CALIFORNIA

Aesculus californica
(Buckeye Family: Hippocastanaceae)

OTHER NAMES: Horse Chestnut

DESCRIPTION: A large bush or tree with a wide round top. Wide lance-shaped leaflets are in groups of 5-7. Flowers are borne in a dense scrub-brush shape at the end of the branches. The most distinctive feature are the baseball size seeds with their shiny mahogany luster offset by a white eye. The seeds are contained in a leathery green pouch while still on the tree. This pouch splits to release the seed at maturity.

HABITAT: Woodlands and hillsides, especially stream banks.

CAUTION: ***Buckeye contains the toxic principle, aesculin. Aesculin imparts a bitter flavor which is usually enough warning to prevent a person from consuming a lethal dose. But, even with the unpleasant taste, children have died after consuming the shiny brown seeds.***

Bees relying on Buckeye for nectar are thought to produce a toxic honey.

USES: The California Indians learned how to remove the toxic principle from Buckeye and used the treated seeds as a food source. The Indians would remove the brown coat from the seed and roast it in an earth oven. The resultant meal would then be placed in baskets and leached in a running stream for up to ten days. Not having the advantage of a running stream, I have tried a modified leaching program to render the seeds edible.

First I strip the outer brown seed coat. The inner portion has somewhat the consistency of a raw potato. Quarter these pieces which are then placed in a pot with 4 volumes of water (the more water the better). The water is boiled and poured off, followed by fresh water and boiling again. This procedure is repeated a total of 8 times. To assure that the aesculin poison has time to leach from the inner tissue, I let the Buckeye potatoes soak overnight between several boilings. This results in the procedure taking 3 days. After leaching the final product will have a very bland taste with all the bitterness removed.

Traditionally, the Indians would consume the leached Buckeye meal without any further preparation.

INTERESTING FACTS: Buckeye seeds were used by the Indians to catch fish. A basket of the seeds would be mashed into a pulp and thrown into a pool. The poisonous principle stupefies the fish which then float to the surface, still alive and easily captured by hand.

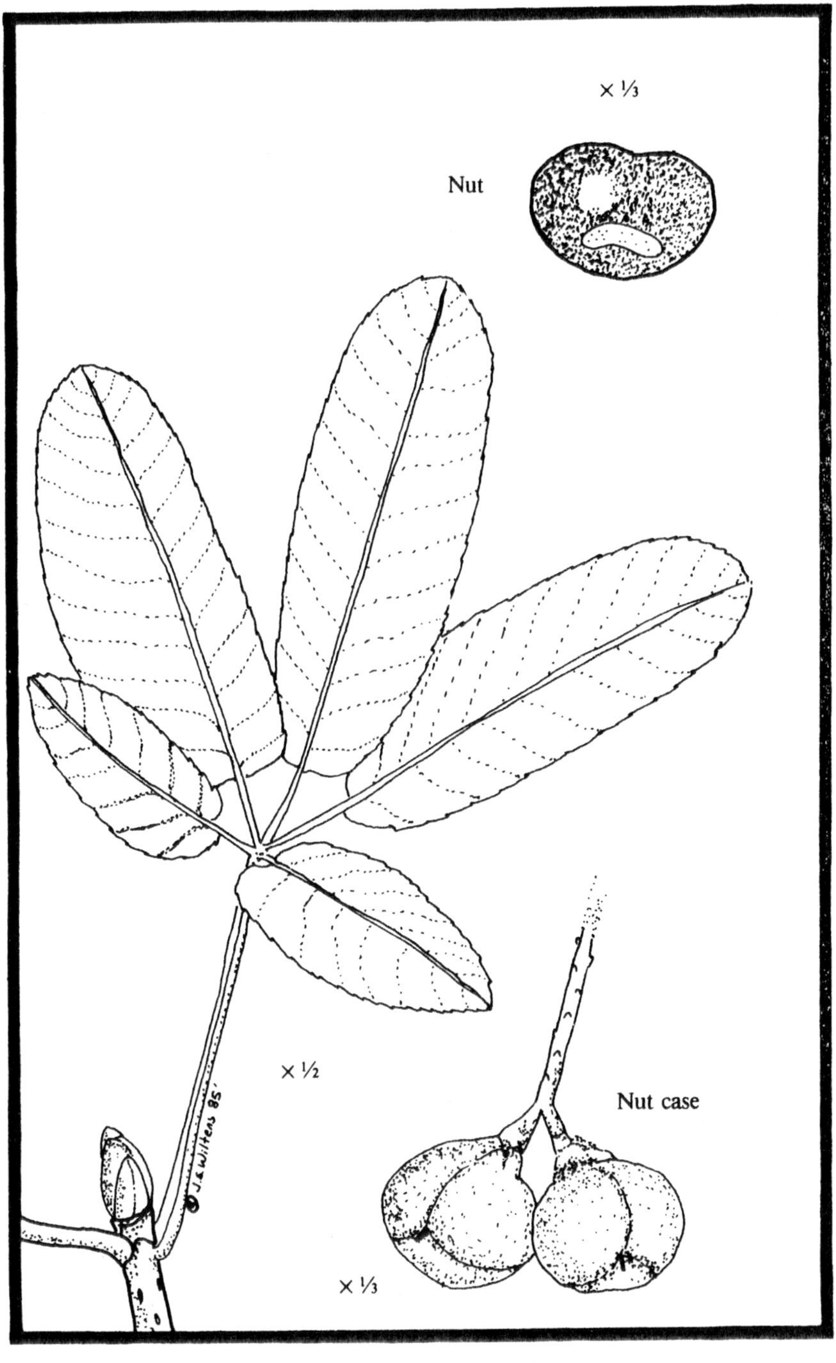

Buckeye (*Aesculus californica*)

BUTTERCUP

Ranunculus repens
(Crowfoot Family: Ranunculaceae)

OTHER NAMES: Creeping Buttercup, Butter Daisy

DESCRIPTION: Partially erect, stems commonly grow horizontally along the ground. Leaflets commonly in groups of three, margins of the leaflets are toothed and lobed. The yellow flowers have 5 petals with a distinctive glossy or varnished look.

HABITAT: Low wet pastures and meadows.

CAUTIONS: ***The juice from Buttercups has been shown to cause ulceration of the skin and severe intestinal upset. The poisonous principle is thought to be protoanemonin. In severe cases it has been implicated in the poisoning of cattle.***

INTERESTING FACTS: When cattle are fed dried hay that contains Buttercups, there is no apparent problem. Drying releases the volatile poison found in the plant, rendering it safe for livestock.

Beggars used to rub the juice from the plant over their skin to raise blisters. Hopefully, their pitiful sight would loosen more coins from a compassionate passerby's pockets.

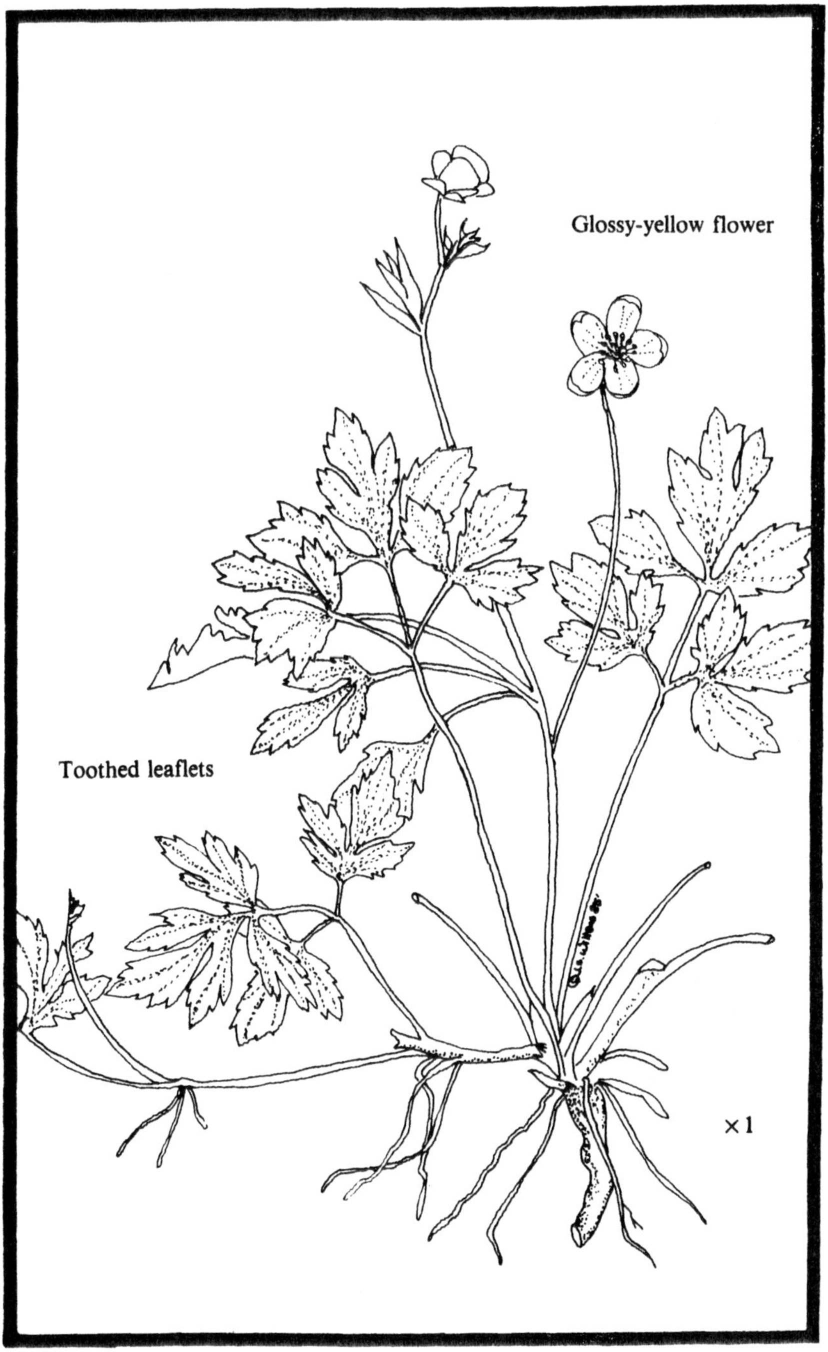

Buttercup, creeping (*Ranunculus repens*)

CAMPHOR TREE

Cinnamomum camphora
(Laurel Family: Lauraceae)

DESCRIPTION: An evergreen tree. The elliptical shaped leaves are bright green on top and a dull green on the underside. Dying leaves turn bright red. The leaves have a distinct camphor odor when crushed. An inconspicuous yellow to white flower. The black fruit is about the size of a pea and contains one seed. Fruits occur in groups of two on a 'Y' shaped branchlet.

HABITAT: Commonly planted in subdivision landscaping.

CAUTION: ***This is the tree from which the substance camphor is obtained. In its purified state, camphor has been used as a pain reliever, to expel worms, as a heart stimulant and an antiseptic. People have eaten the leaves to create a camphor high, a potentially dangerous use of the plant. Children should be warned not to eat the berries.***

INTERESTING FACTS: Camphor trees are related to the trees which produce cinnamon.

If you have a problem with odor from perspiring feet, try putting several camphor leaves in your shoes.

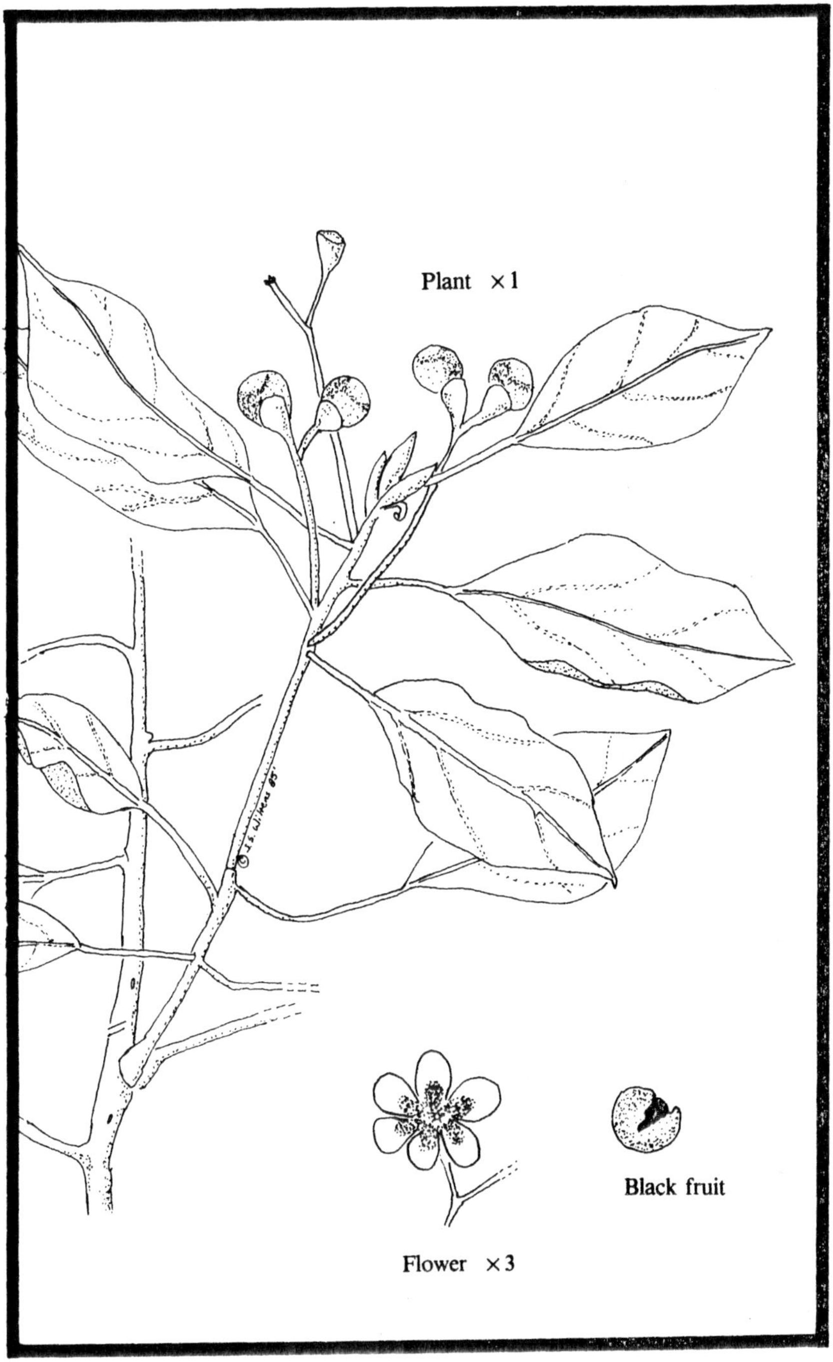

Camphor Tree (*Cinnamomum camphora*)

CASTOR BEAN

Ricinus communis
(Spurge Family: Euphorbiaceae)

OTHER NAMES: Castor Oil Plant.

DESCRIPTION: A tree-like shrub up to 12 feet tall. The large palm-shaped leaves have 5-11 lobes and a saw-toothed margin. Flowers are borne on a spike with red female flowers above yellow male flowers. The spiny fruits contain three seeds each. The seeds are very distinctive with a glossy tan surface mottled with gray or brown.

HABITAT: Disturbed areas, roadsides, sometimes planted as an ornamental.

CAUTION: ***This plant is a potential killer. All parts of the plant contain the phytotoxin, ricin, a severe irritant. The poison is especially concentrated in the seeds. As little as 1 seed can kill a child, while 3 seeds may kill an adult.***

While living in Hawaii I heard of servicemen there using an old folk remedy, swallowing one or two seeds whole as a laxative. When you consider how potent ricin is, 0.01 milligrams can kill an adult, I was somewhat amazed that this folk remedy had not killed these men. It turns out that if the seed coats are not broken, the seed may pass through the digestive tract unopened. Unknown to these members of the armed forces, just one cracked seed and they could have become seriously ill.

Visitors across the border often return with necklaces made from the attractive Castor Bean seeds. Periodically the news media issues a warning that chewing or sucking on the pierced seeds in these necklaces can cause illness or death.

INTERESTING FACTS: Castor oil is derived from Castor Bean. It has a long standing use as a laxative. The reason that castor oil is not toxic is due to the fact that ricin is not soluble in oil. It is also destroyed by heat. Castor oil is made by dry roasting the seeds for 1 hour, pressing out the oil, mixing the oil with water and boiling and finally skimming off the processed oil.

In Russia, large tracts of Castor Bean were once grown to produce an oil lubricant used on airplanes. Castor oil does not readily freeze in harsh climates making it preferred to other lubricants.

The poison, ricin, from Castor Beans, was used to assassinate a BBC broadcaster critical of the Bulgarian government. The poison was chosen because of its high toxicity. The method of delivery was injection in pellet form from the tip of an umbrella.

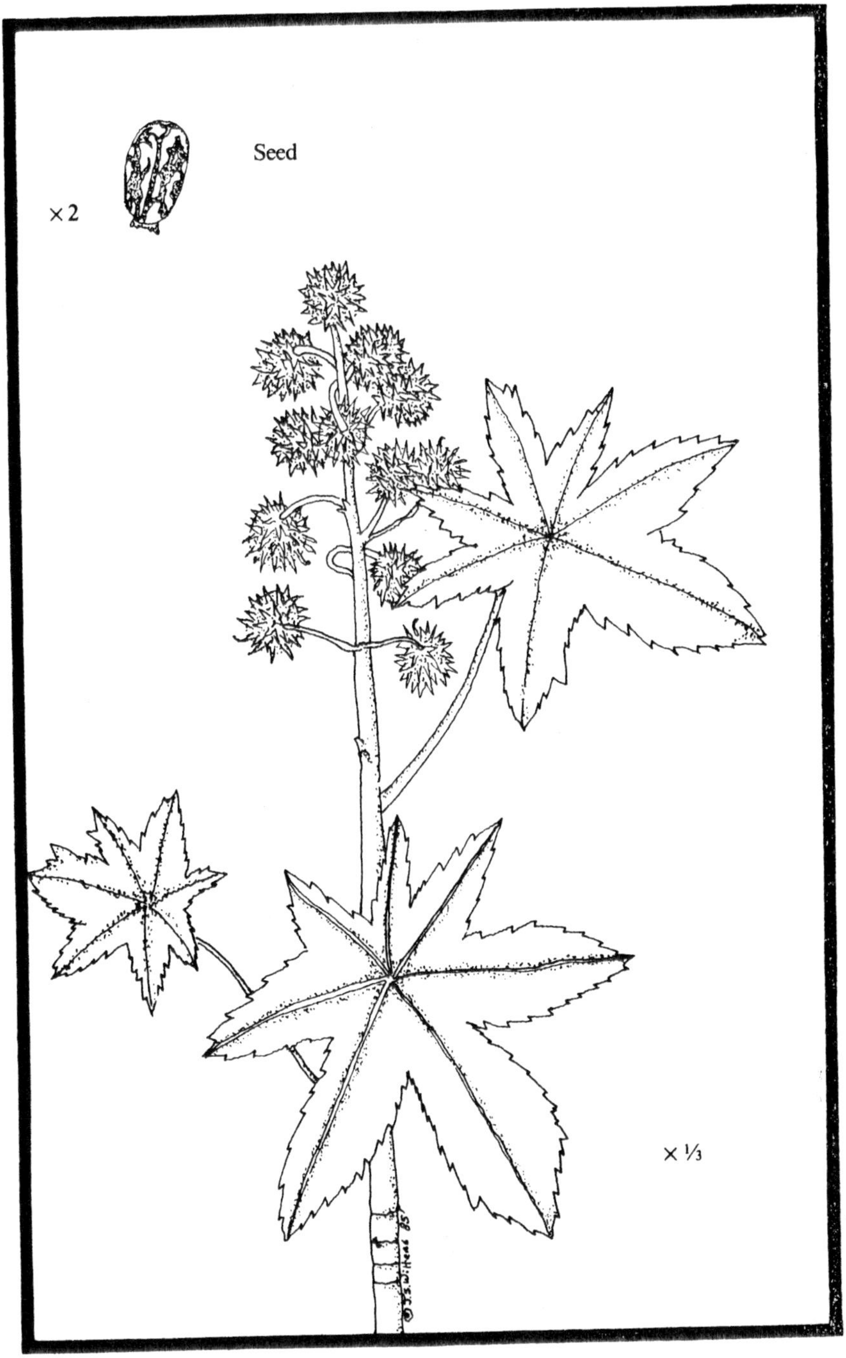

Castor Bean (Ricinus communis)

COCKLEBUR

Xanthium strumarium
(Sunflower Family: Compositae)

OTHER NAMES: Clot-Burr, Sheep Burr.

DESCRIPTION: Stout branching stems often discolored with purple dots or lines. Leaves borne on leaf stalks spaced alternately up the stem. Broad leaves with coarsely indented margins. The burrs are covered with prickles and two stout horns or hooks at the end.

HABITAT: Waste areas, vacant lots, fields.

CAUTION: ***This plant contains the toxic glucoside, xanthostrumarin. It is most prevalent in the germinating seeds and young plants.***

Cattle that have consumed Cocklebur show signs of nausea and vomiting. If they consume sufficient amounts of the plant it can lead to death.

I have included this plant because it is sometimes confused with another plant, Burdock (*Arctium minus* and *lappa*). The general leaf shape and the presence of burrs gives them a similarity that can be confusing. This is also the reason for deleting Burdock from the edible portion of this book. As I explained in the introduction, beginners should avoid using edible plants that can be readily confused with poisonous look-a-likes.

INTERESTING FACTS: If you ever lose a button on a backpacking trip, try using one of the burrs as a substitute. They are the original Velcro, being especially tenacious on wool shirts and long-haired dogs. Someone once told me, rather facetiously, that the only way you can get Cockleburs off an Irish setter is to, "wet the dog down regular, and when them burrs spring up into little plants, pull them up — roots and all."

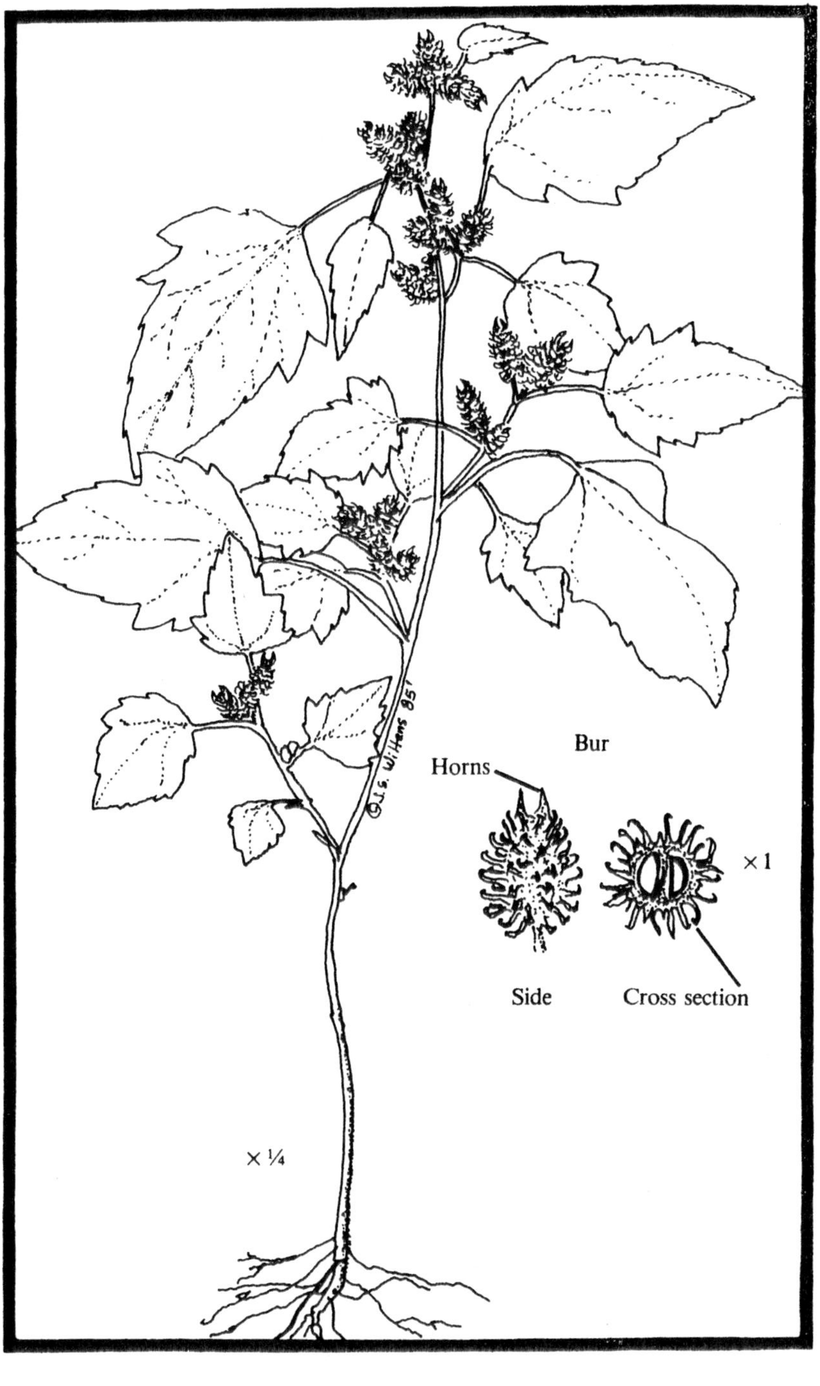

Cocklebur (*Xanthium strumarium*)

IVY

Hedera helix
(Ginseng Family: Araliaceae)

OTHER NAMES: English Ivy, Algerian Ivy.

DESCRIPTION: Trailing vines, sometimes becoming woody and thickened. Either climbing or low ground cover forms. Leaves are spade shaped, some with a smooth margin, others have 3-5 lobes. The greenish flowers occur in round clusters on a terminal stem. The flowers, after fertilization, are replaced with hard black 3-5 seeded berries.

HABITAT: Abandoned areas, common as a ground cover and climbing trellises in gardens.

CAUTION: ***Contains a glucoside poison, hederin. The foliage is the most poisonous, but the berries also contain the toxin. Consuming the plant can cause severe digestive upset and, in extreme cases, death.***

Some people experience a contact dermatitis when handling ivy.

INTERESTING FACTS: Long before neon signs, a garland of ivy hanging above a doorway designated a tavern. This was probably based on an association of Ivy with Bacchus, the god of wine.

Ivy leaves were once boiled and mashed into a dark fluid that was utilized to revitalize black silk.

Climbing Ivy has hair-like tendrils on the stem which modify into rootlets on contact with the proper substrate. Ivy can climb as high as 80-90 feet under good conditions.

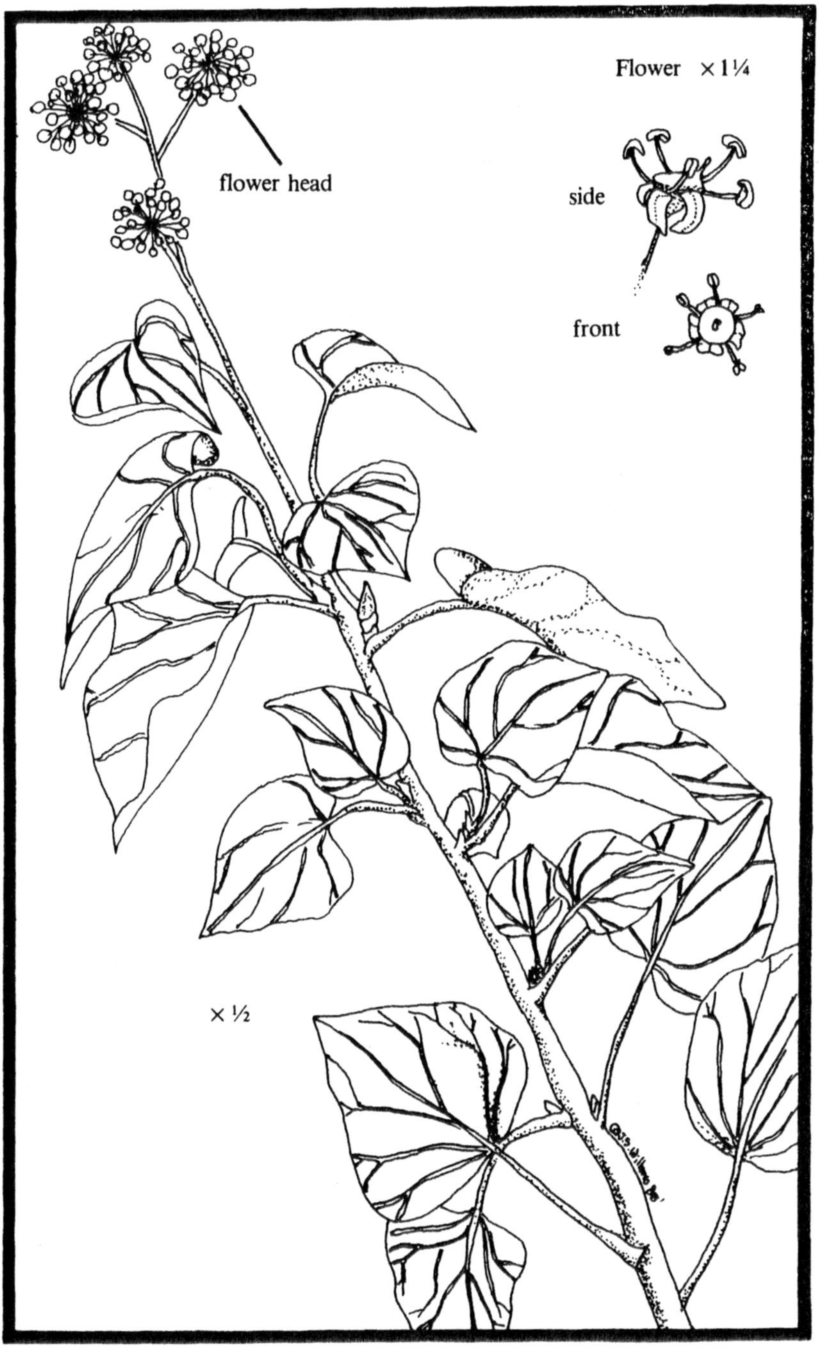

Ivy (*Hedera helix*)

JIMSONWEED

Datura meteloides **and** ***stramonium***
(Nightshade Family: Solanaceae)

OTHER NAMES: Thornapple, Jamestown-Weed, Stinkweed.

DESCRIPTION: Waist-high herb. Thick erect stems have widely spaced branches in *D. meteloides* and sparse branching in *D. stramonium.* Leaves are alternate, ovate in outline, with an uneven coarsely toothed margin. The leaves are green to purple with a rancid peanut-butter odor. Large five-toothed trumpet shaped flowers may be white or tinged with violet. The fruit is spherical in *D. meteloides* and egg-shaped in *D. stramonium.*Both species have a collar shaped structure attached to the fruit. Initially the spiny fruits are fleshy, as the season progresses the fruits dry and split to release the seeds.

HABITAT: Waste places, vacant lots, orchards and pastures.

CAUTION: ***All parts of the plant are poisonous. It contains such alkaloid poisons as hyoscyamine, atropine and hyoscine. Hyoscine is also known as scopolamine, a hallucinogen. In California, adults have died from consuming a liquid brewed from the leaves of the plant, and children have died after eating the seeds.***

The interest in this plant has stemmed from its early use as a narcotic. Various California Indian tribes utilized the plant in puberty rites to gain visions. Carlos Castaneda, in his book, "Teachings of Don Juan," describes the Indian ceremonial rites employing Datura.

Medical authorities have cautioned that use of Datura as a recreational drug involves severe risk to the user. Depending on dosage and sensitivity the patient may experience a progressive set of very unpleasant symptoms: elevated temperature as high as 104°F., impaired vision, loss of coordination, incoherence, hallucinations, possible violent seizures, coma and death. Even among the experienced native Indian tribes of California, there were occasional deaths due to improper dosages of the plant.

INTERESTING FACTS: The common name, Jimsonweed, was derived from Jamestown. In 1676 there was a mass poisoning of residents of Jamestown Virginia when they mistakenly used the plant as a potherb.

In South America the Chilocha tribe in Columbia used a concotion of Datura to drug wives prior to burying them alive with their deceased husbands.

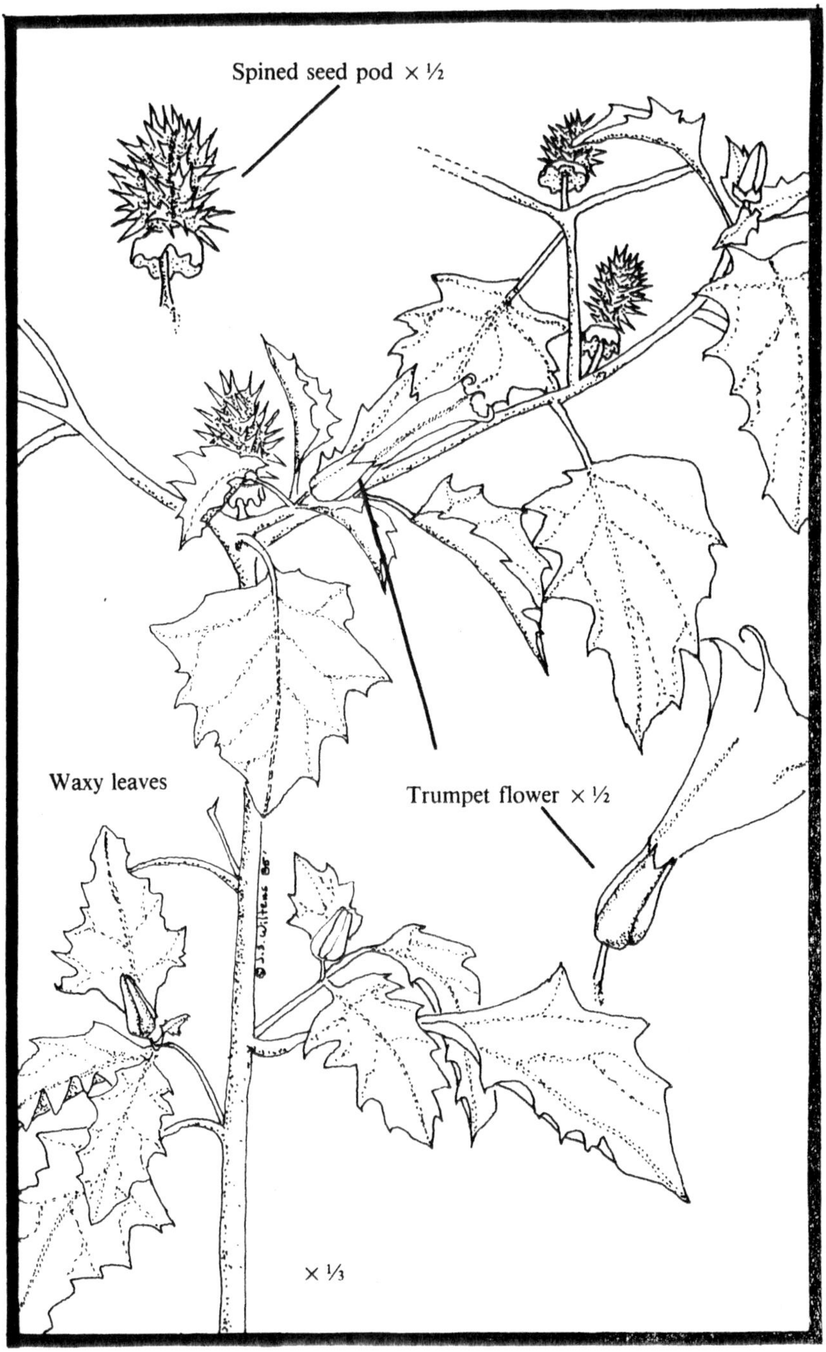

Jimsonweed (*Datura stramonium*)

In India and England, the plant has been used by thugs and prostitutes to render their victims helpless prior to relieving them of their valuables.

The drug, scopolamine, found in *Datura sps*, is used in a new motion sickness preventative. The remedy, manufactured by Alza Corporation here in Santa Clara Valley, is transferred through the skin by a transdermal disk. Considering that scopolamine is the hallucinogenic constituent in Jimsonweed, you might expect some potential problems with it in a motion sickness formula. A physician relayed to me the story of an elderly lady with an intolerance to the drug. Apparently a grandmother affixed a disk to her skin prior to an airplane flight. While enroute she proceeded to remove all her clothes and then tried to walk about the plane showing pictures of her grandchildren to fellow passengers.

LUPINE

Lupinus sps.
(Pea Family: Leguminosae)

OTHER NAMES: Wolf Pea, Blue Pea, Indian Beans

DESCRIPTION: This genus contains numerous species. Plants are upright. Leaves are palmately compound (like the fingers of a hand spread wide open) and alternate up the stem. The petals of the flower are fused together and look like a Dutch woman's bonnet. Flowers occur in terminal racemes and may be blue, purple, white, yellow or red. Seeds are contained in flattened pods. The roots are often covered with small bumps or nodules.

HABITAT: Pastures, hillsides, open areas.

CAUTIONS: ***Many species of lupines contain alkaloid poisons that have been responsible for livestock death and poisoning in man. Since it is very difficult to distinguish the poisonous from the non-poisonous lupines, this is a plant that should be avoided. Children often mistake the seed pods for peas, sometimes with fatal results.***

INTERESTING FACTS: The genus name is derived from the Latin, "lupus," a wolf. The name stems from the ancient belief that Lupines, like a wolf, devoured or robbed the soil. In reality, Lupines do just the opposite. If you look at the roots of Lupine, you will often find little bumps. These bumps are nitrogen fixation nodules. The plant has established a symbiotic realationship with a bacterium that lives in the nodules and can fix nitrogen from the air. This is one reason the Lupine is often found growing on very poor soils, it can manufacture its own fertilizer. Contrary to ancient man's belief, this plant actually enriches the soil.

There is an interesting theory that Lupine may have contributed to class distinctions in the past. The upper classes were usually able to assure food on their tables even in times of famine. Poor people would have to make do with whatever they could find. Lupine was often turned to in times of crisis and the seeds were used in gruel. Some Lupines, which are recorded in old herbals as being edible, have been shown to contain toxic principles. The poisonous principle was not enough to cause obvious discomfort but may have contributed to minor brain damage over a prolonged period of use. The "Lupine-eaters" would seem a bit more "stupid" than the rest of the populace. This would be an example of a dietary problem restricting the upward mobility of a poorer class.

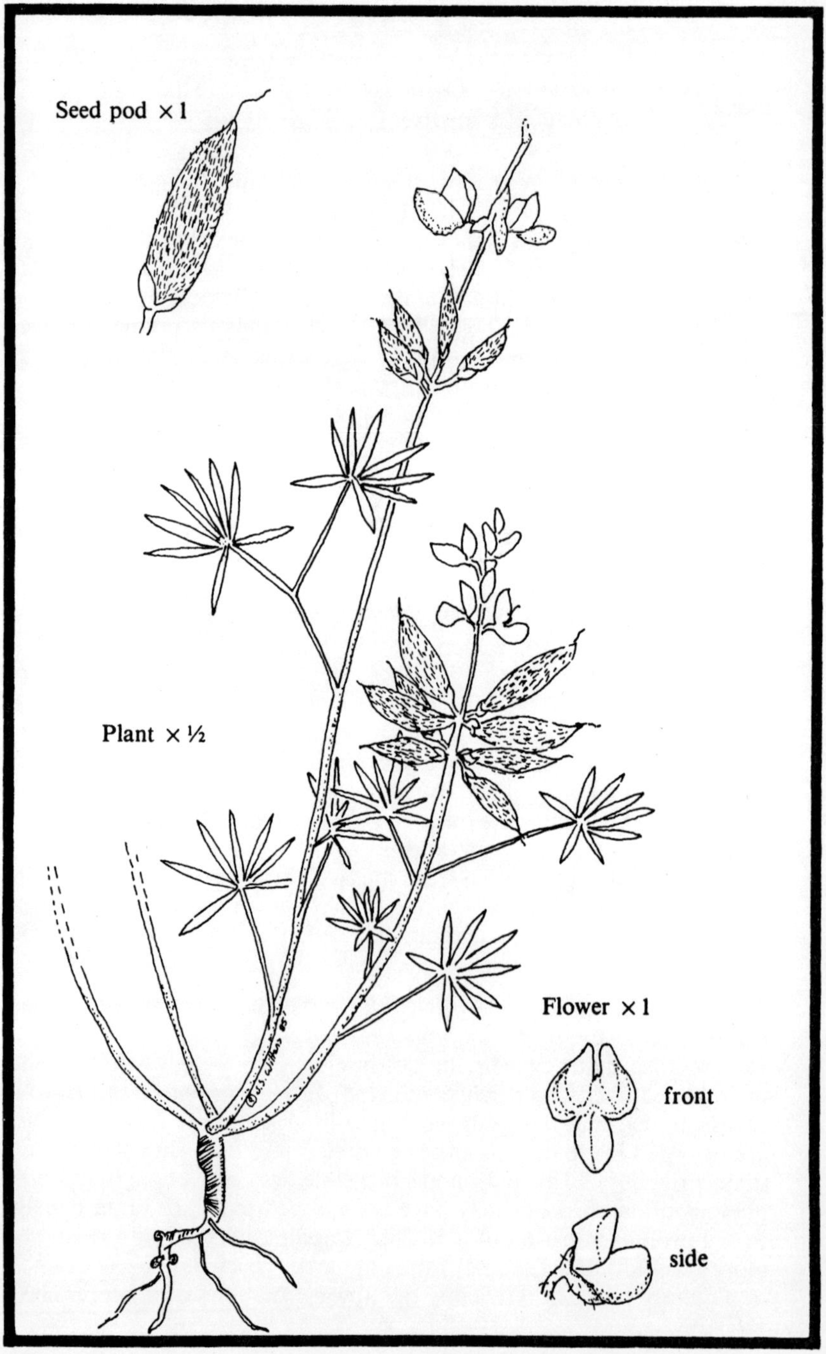

Lupine (*Lupinus sp.*)

MISTLETOE

Phoradendron flavescens var. villosum
(Mistletoe Family: Loranthaceae)

DESCRIPTION: Parasitic plants often found on Oaks. The brittle stems are attached directly to the branches of a host tree. The thick pad-like leaves are opposite, oval to broadly lance-shaped, covered with a tight fuzz with a dull green coloration. Berries are BB sized, translucent white to yellowish clusters arising at the leaf-stem axis.

HABITAT: Found growing mostly on Oak trees.

CAUTIONS: ***Mistletoe contains the toxic amines, beta-phenylethylamine and tyramine. Children have died after consuming the berries. Tea brewed from the leaves has proved toxic.***

It is interesting to note that some animals such as pigs and goats have eaten species of Mistletoe with apparent impunity, while cattle in California have died from eating the leaves.

INTERESTING FACTS: The technical name for Mistletoe, *Phoradendron*, comes from the Greek: 'phor', a thief, and 'dendron', tree. This plant is truly a thief. It taps its root system into a host tree and draws its nourishment directly from the tree's sap.

Birds regularly eat Mistletoe berries. This is a good example of an old wives' tale. Contrary to the wives' tales, what another animal can eat is not necessarily safe for humans.

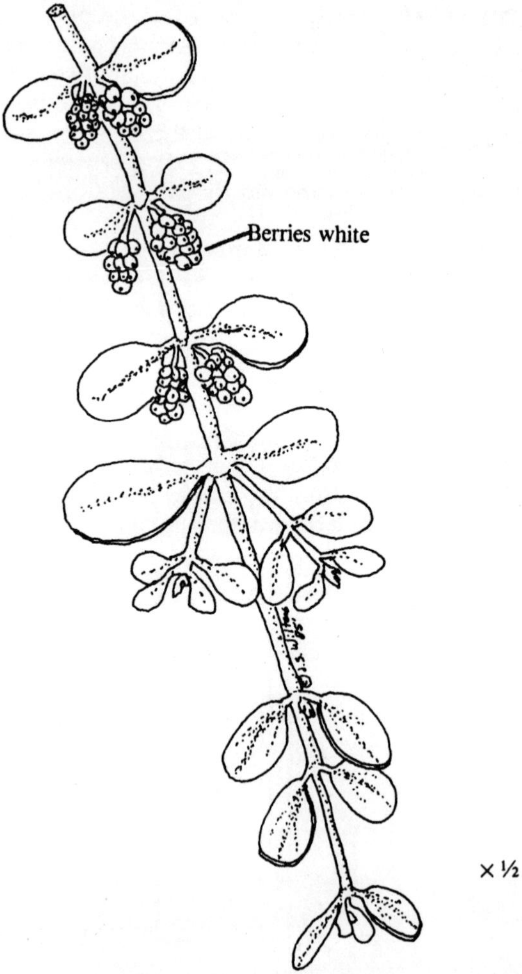

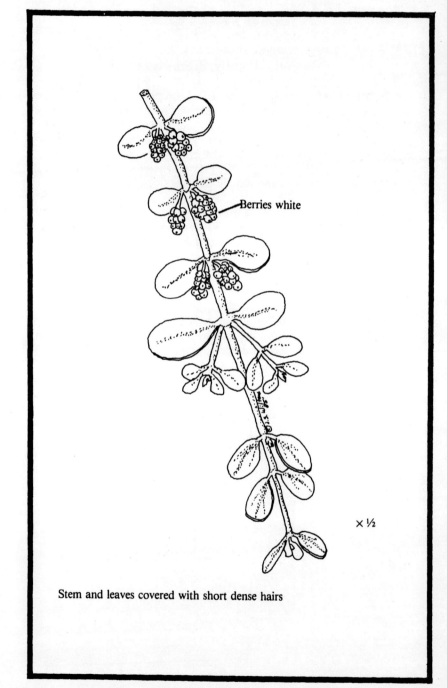

Stem and leaves covered with short dense hairs

Mistletoe (*Phoradendron flavescens var. villosum*)

MORNING GLORY

Ipomoea tricolor
(Morning Glory Family: Convolvulaceae)

DESCRIPTION: Twining climbing vines. Large heart shaped leaves. Showy funnel shaped flowers with a range of colors depending on variety: blue, lavender, pink, red and white. Bear a large number of round capsular seed pods.

HABITAT: Gardens, waste areas and vacant lots.

CAUTION: ***Morning Glory seeds contain alkaloids and LSD-like compounds. During the 60's, when drug experimentation was the craze, amateur pharmacologists would prepare potent brews of pulverized seeds. Unfortunately a number of these human guinea pigs experienced more than hallucinations; sometimes nausea, convulsions and death followed their tests.***

The amount of potent material in seeds is variable, dependent on growing conditions and the variety of Morning Glory. As a ball park figure, about 50 mashed or well chewed seeds has proven potent.

INTERESTING FACTS: The seed coat of the Morning Glory is so tough that it is a hindrance to its own germination. Commercial growers often sell scarified seeds to assist germination.

The Aztecs were known to use several members of the Convolvulaceae family, among them Morning Glory, to induce psychic religious visions. When the Spaniards gained control, they banned the use of the mind-altering seeds because of the satanic-visions produced.

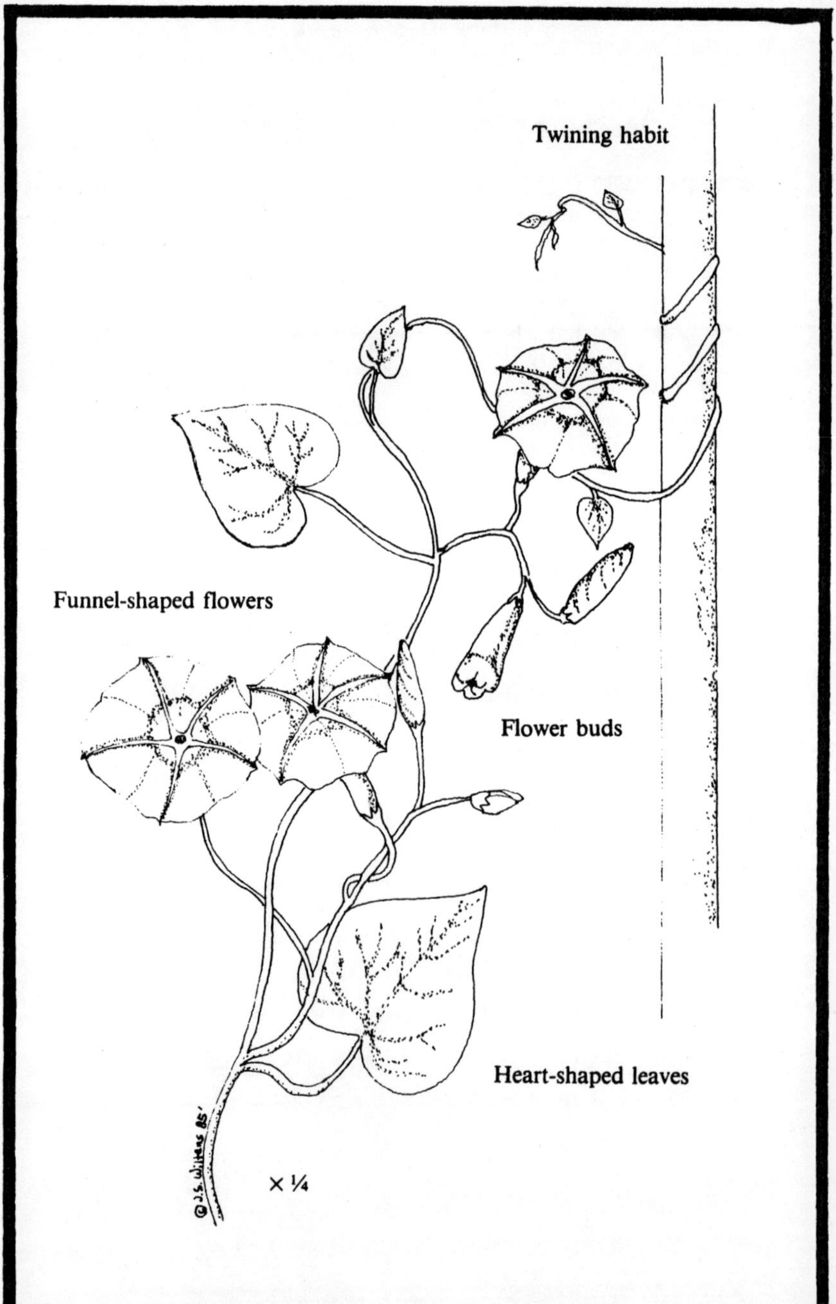

Morning Glory (*Ipomoea tricolor*)

NIGHTSHADE, CLIMBING

Solanum dulcamara
(Nightshade Family: Solanaceae)

OTHER NAMES: Bittersweet, Blue Nightshade

DESCRIPTION: A woody climbing, vine like plant. Leaves may have a simple spear-head shape or may also include several lobes at the leaf base. The 5 petaled flowers are blue to lavender with a distinctive beak protruding from the center. The grape sized berries are orange to red.

HABITAT: Along stream banks, hedges and thickets.

CAUTION: ***Many members of the nightshade family are toxic. This species contains an alkaloid glucoside, solanine. The attractive red berries have been consumed by children with fatal results.***

INTERESTING FACTS: The genus name *Solanum* is derived from the Latin word, 'solanem', which means quieting. Nightshade poisons have a quieting or narcotic effect upon the respiratory system.

A poison derived from Nightshade species may have been what Shakespeare had in mind when the priest, in Romeo and Juliet, gave Juliet a draught which would give her the semblance of death.

The Nightshade family also contains a number of edible plants, among them the potato and tomato. Though we usually consider the potato and tomato rather benign vegetables, they are toxic — if you eat the wrong portion. The green vines and fruit of the potato are toxic as are the stems and leaves of the tomato. It probably took primitive man some time to figure out which portions of certain plants were edible. In the case of the tomato, Europeans commonly believed it to be poisonous up into the 17th century. Even in the United States, it was not until Thomas Jefferson made a public display of eating tomatoes that they became a commonly accepted table vegetable.

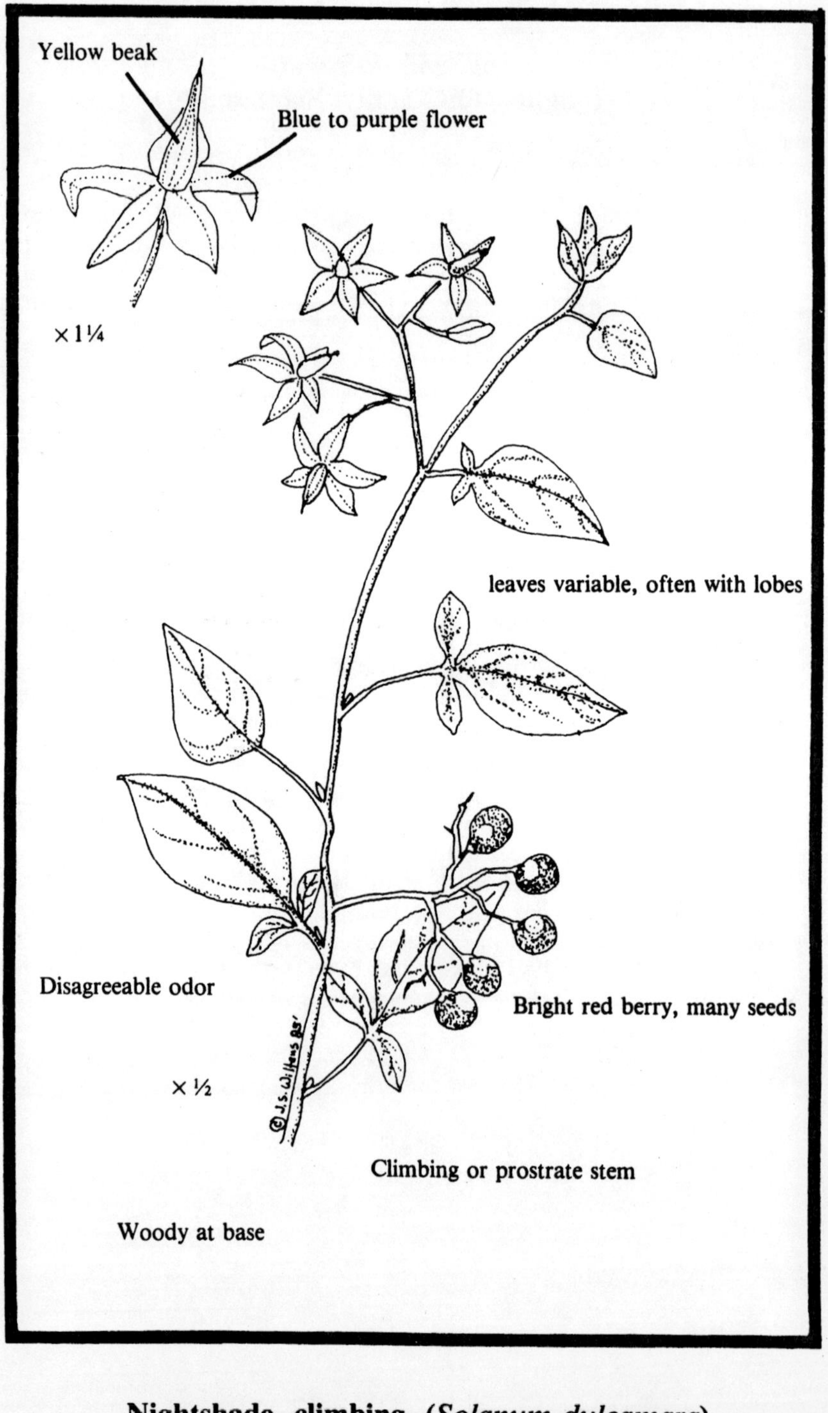

Nightshade, climbing (*Solanum dulcamara*)

OLEANDER

Nerium oleander
(Dogbane Family: Apocynaceae)

DESCRIPTION: Stout evergreen shrub. Leaves of Oleander are lance shaped, dark green with a distinctive midrib, leathery and glossy. Leaves are opposite or in whorls of three. Showy flowers appear clustered at the tips of branches. They may be white to pink to dark red. Cigar shaped seed pods.

HABITAT: Common in freeway divider strips and hedge plantings.

CAUTION: ***The dogbane family is renown for its toxic members. The term dogbane refers to some plants in this family being used to reduce the dog population. Oleander contains over 50 toxic compounds, which include cardiac glycosides and alkaloids. Consuming as little as a single leaf can prove fatal for a child, whereas 3 leaves can kill an adult. The plant is poisonous both fresh and dried.***

The plant is so toxic that just using the wood as a skewer for meat has killed. In one case an army of French troops used Oleander skewers for a barbecue, 300 men were poisoned and a number died. Unwary picnickers in California have achieved the same result.

It's unwise to burn Oleander clippings since the poisonous principle is carried on the smoke particles and if inhaled could cause poisoning.

INTERESTING FACTS: Domesticated animals have been poisoned on a number of occasions from eating Oleander, yet one of this plant's ornamental attributes is the fact that deer will not feed on it. It would be curious to find out how deer got so smart.

One of the strange symptoms of Oleander poisoning is a visual perception change. Apparently yellow and green colors along with geometric shapes appear around objects.

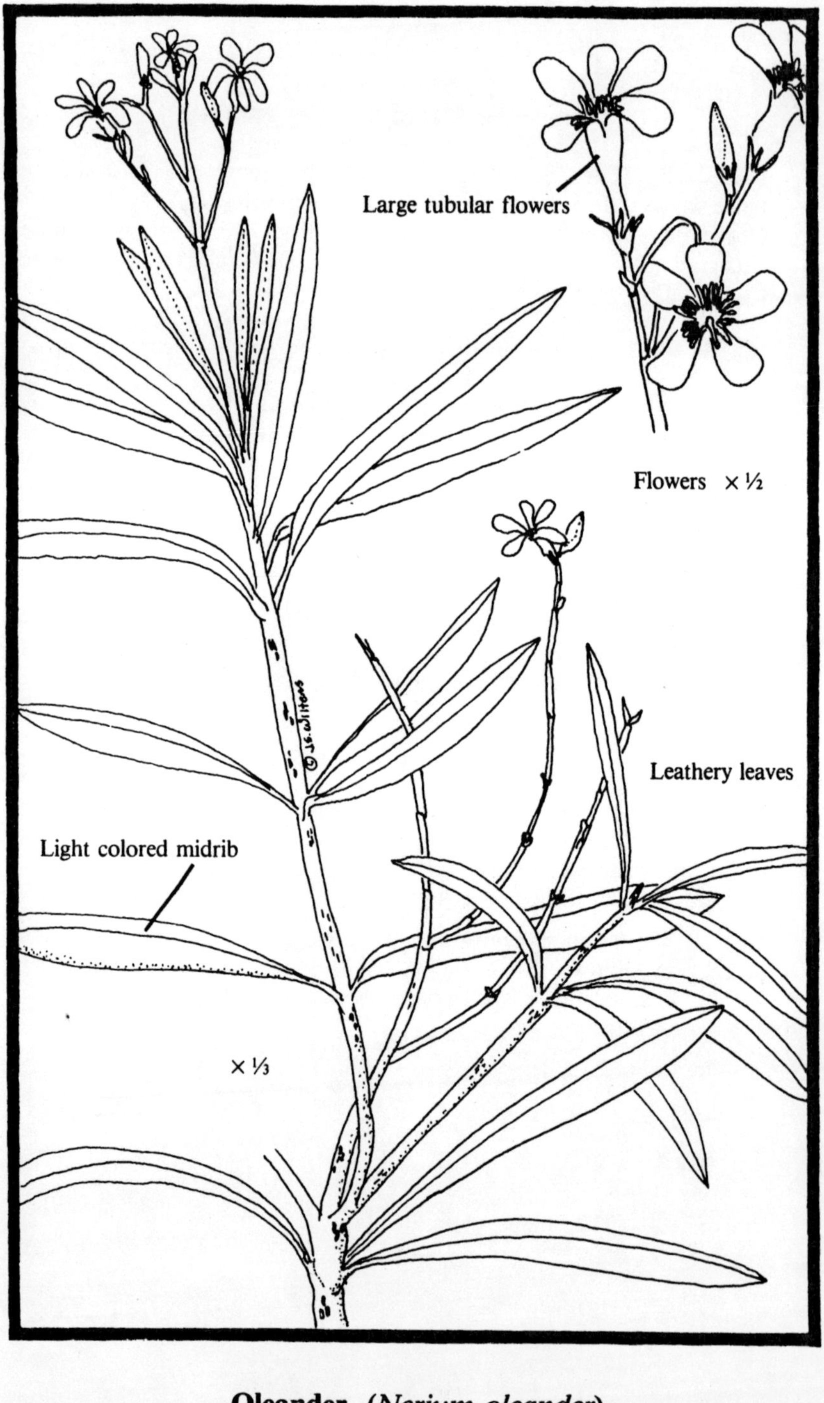

Oleander (*Nerium oleander*)

PEPPER TREE, CALIFORNIA

Schinus molle
(Sumac Family: Anacardiaceae)

OTHER NAMES: Australian Pepper

DESCRIPTION: Tree up to 45 feet high. Long hanging twigs give it a weeping willow look. Small scythe-shaped leaves alternate on the twigs. Yellowish white flowers. The faded red berries contain a single seed and hang in pendulous clusters.

HABITAT: Common in freeway planter strips.

CAUTION: ***Reputed to be poisonous.***

INTERESTING FACTS: This tree is commonly found planted along freeway margins due to its drought resistance. The root system spreads long distances under ground in search of water. Due to its pervasive root growth it is not an appreciated plant in sidewalk planting or near septic tanks since it can lift concrete and clog leach fields.

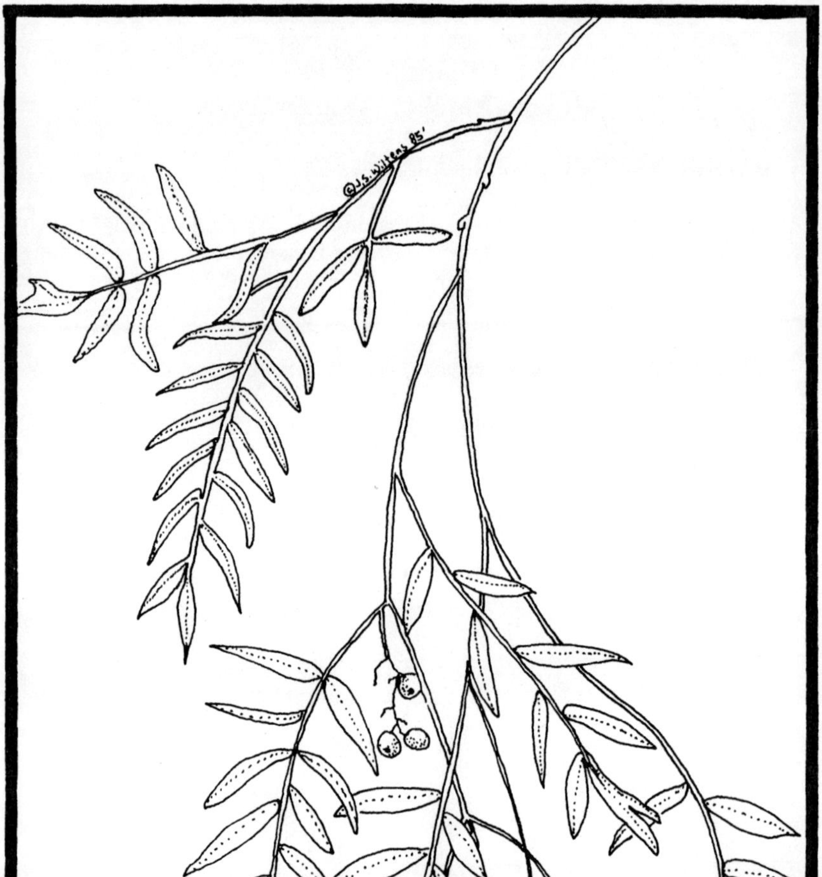

Pepper tree (*Schinus molle*)

POISON HEMLOCK

Conium maculatum
(Carrot Family: Umbelliferae)

OTHER NAMES: Fool's Parsley, California Fern

DESCRIPTION: The smooth upright hollow stems are blotched with purple. It is important to note that the stems of Poison Hemlock are hairless. The leaf stalks clasp the stem. The leaves appear fern-like with numerous small divisions. The small white flowers occur in flat-topped clusters. The root looks like a small white carrot. If a portion of the plant is crushed it has a very unpleasant odor.

HABITAT: Vacant lots, meadows, stream banks, old fields and ditches.

CAUTION: ***This is a serious poisonous plant. It has been implicated in many deaths, the most notorious being the poisoning of Socrates.*** From the *Phaedo* we have this description of the symptoms of Socrates' poisoning:
Then Crito made a sign to his slave, who was standing by, and the slave went out, and...returned with the man who was to give the poison, carrying it prepared in a cup. When Socrates saw him, he asked, "You understand these things, my good sir, what have I to do?" "You have only to drink this," he replied...Socrates...put the cup to his lips and drank the poison quite...cheerfully. He walked about, until he said that his legs were getting heavy, and then he lay down on his back....The man who gave the poison began to examine his feet and legs, from time to time: then he pressed his foot hard, and asked if there was any feeling in it; and Socrates said, "No:" and then his legs, and so higher and higher, and showed us that he was cold and stiff. And Socrates felt himself, and said that when it came to his heart, he should be gone, He was already growing cold about the groin, when he uncovered his face which had been covered, and spoke for the last time. "Crito," he said, "I owe a cock to Asclepius: do not forget to pay it." "It shall be done," replied Crito. "Is there anything else that you wish?" He made no answer to this question; but after a short interval there was no movement, and the man uncovered him, and his eyes were fixed. Then Crito closed his mouth and his eyes.

A friend relayed a story about how toxic Poison Hemlock can be. While taking a botany class, one of the students touched some Hemlock to her tongue and then spit it out. A half hour later she was taken to a hospital, complaining of a numbness in her legs.

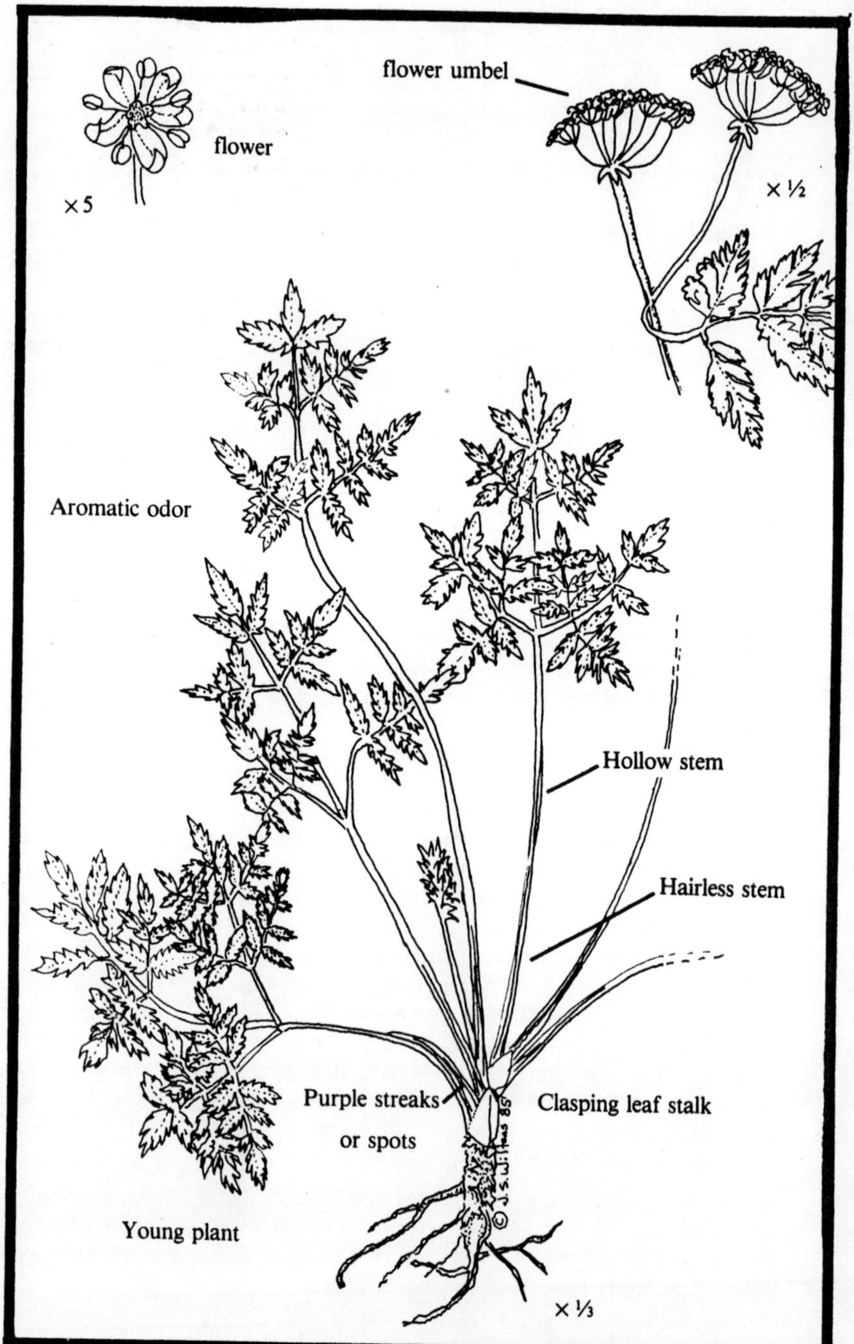

Poison Hemlock (*Conium maculatum*)

This plant is widespread in California and accidental poisoning occurs regularly. Poisoning has occurred from confusing the seeds for anise, the leaves for parsley and the root for parsnip or wild carrot. Since there are a number of similarities between the edible and deadly members of the carrot family, you must have a thorough understanding of the distinctions between the safe and the potentially fatal plants in this group.

POISON OAK

Rhus diversiloba
previously ***Toxicodendron diversiloba***
(Sumac Family: Anacardiaceae)

OTHER NAMES: Poison Creeper, Three-Leaved Ivy, Poison Ivy.

DESCRIPTION: Usually an erect shrub, there is also a climbing variety with aerial rootlets. Oak-shaped toothed leaflets in groups of three. Color, a light shiny green to dark green to bright red depending on time of year. Small green flowers occur in leaf axils. The poisonous fruits are small white or cream colored berries which hang in clusters. Field conditions often result in quite a variation in plant form from one locale to another.

HABITAT: Hillsides, open forests, pastures, stream banks.

CAUTION: ***This is one plant that every outdoor person should know. Like most people, I learned about Poison Oak the hard way. Merely contacting the leaves or twigs can cause an irritating rash and blisters.*** The poisonous principle is a mixture of oleoresins, commonly referred to as urishols. Merely being in the presence of Poison Oak will not cause the rash. You must touch the plant or another object that has contacted the plant such as clothing, tools or the family pet.

Also be aware that the smoke from burning Poison Oak can cause irritation, particularly serious if it gets in the eyes or is inhaled.

Many people claim immunity to Poison Oak. Though there may be individuals who will not experience sensitization to this plant, repeated exposure increases the possibility of sensitization. If you contact the plant, wash with a strong soap (one without an oil base, as such soaps tend to spread the urishol poison). You should wash within 10 minutes of contacting the plant. Another possibility is washing the affected part with a 5% solution of ferric chloride in a 50:50 mix of alcohol and water. Even if you wash shortly after contact, you may still have a reaction, but washing helps to prevent the spread of the oils and will contain the rash.

There are a host of old wives' tales and remedies concerning Poison Oak. Remember that what may work for one person may be very hazardous for another, such as the suggestion: if you eat a Poison Oak leaf it will make you immune. This prescription to gain immunity has resulted in serious consequences. The mucous membranes of the throat may swell rapidly causing suffocation not to mention a number of gastrointestinal problems.

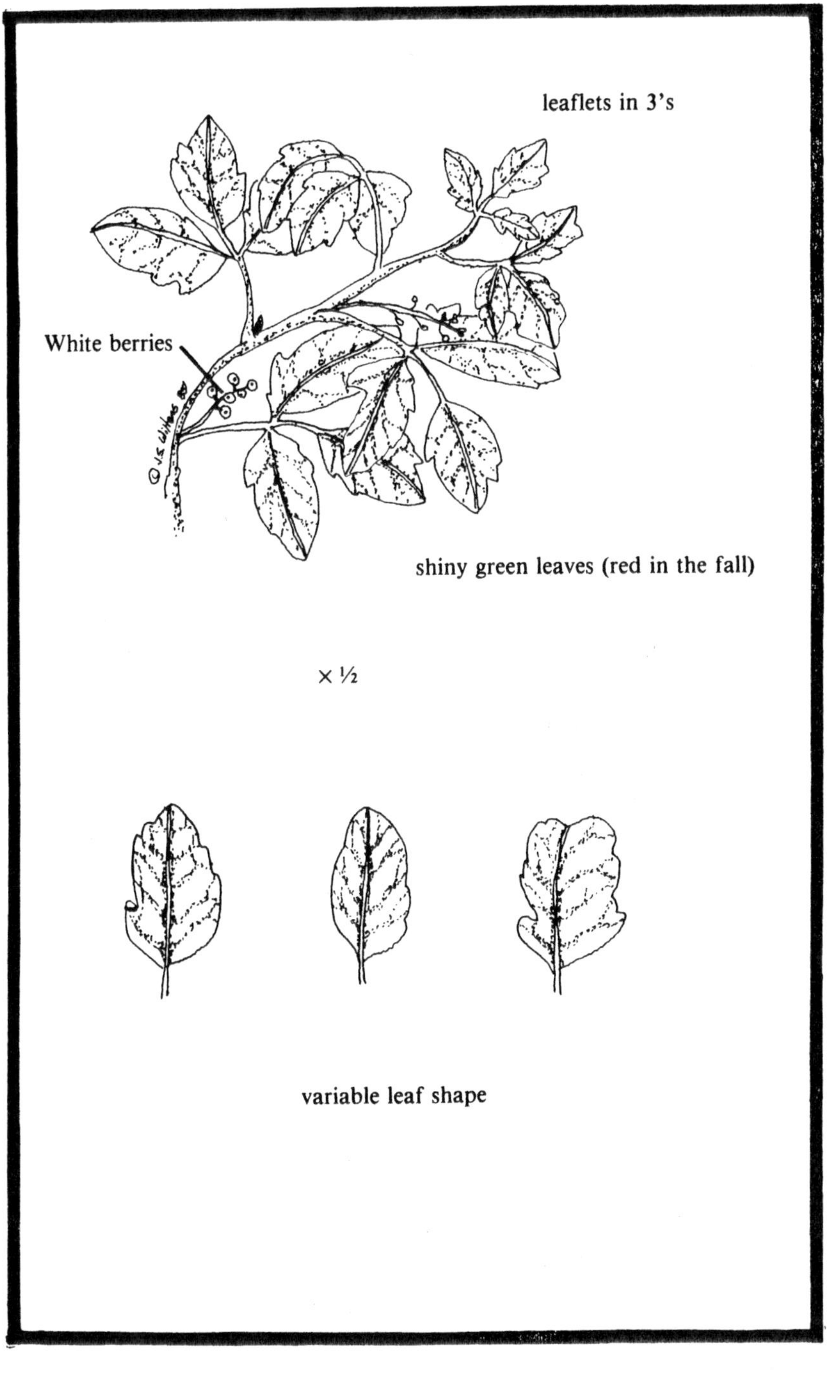

Poison Oak (*Rhus diversiloba*)

INTERESTING FACTS: Native California Indians used Poison Oak with apparent immunity. It was used in fire pits to cover baked foods, their roots were used in basket weaving (often with great discomfort to white men who handled such baskets) and a dye was made from the sap. Any cross-breeding with the white man apparently resulted in a loss of immunity.

When I was in the process of locating a site for a children's summer camp, Deer Crossing Camp Inc., one of my criteria was that it should be at an elevation of 3500 feet or higher. Poison Oak is rarely found above 3500 feet. The site finally chosen sits at 6500 feet in the Sierra, quite safe from the problems of Poison Oak.

SCOURING RUSH

Equisetum arvense
(Horsetail Family: Equisetaceae)

OTHER NAMES: Horsetail

DESCRIPTION: There are two types of upright aerial stems. The hollow cylindrical stems may have thin branchlets occurring in whorls at the joints or there may be no branching in which case the tip will be a blunt bullet shape. The stems have a gritty texture due to the high silica content.

HABITAT: Habitually moist ground around springs, creeks and ponds.

CAUTION: ***Recent books on edible plants occasionally list E. arvense as edible. Some caution needs to be used here as Scouring Rush has been implicated in livestock deaths.*** The nerve poison, aconitic acid, has been found in *Equisetum* sps. as well as thiaminase, an enzyme that breaks down vitamin B_1. Even though heat destroys thiaminase, and a human is not likely to eat as much of this plant as a forage animal, the potential risks do not warrant this plant being on your foraging list.

INTERESTING FACTS: Due to the high silica content, these plants have been used to polish floors and metal. Backpackers have found Scouring Rush to be a very effective pot scrubber.

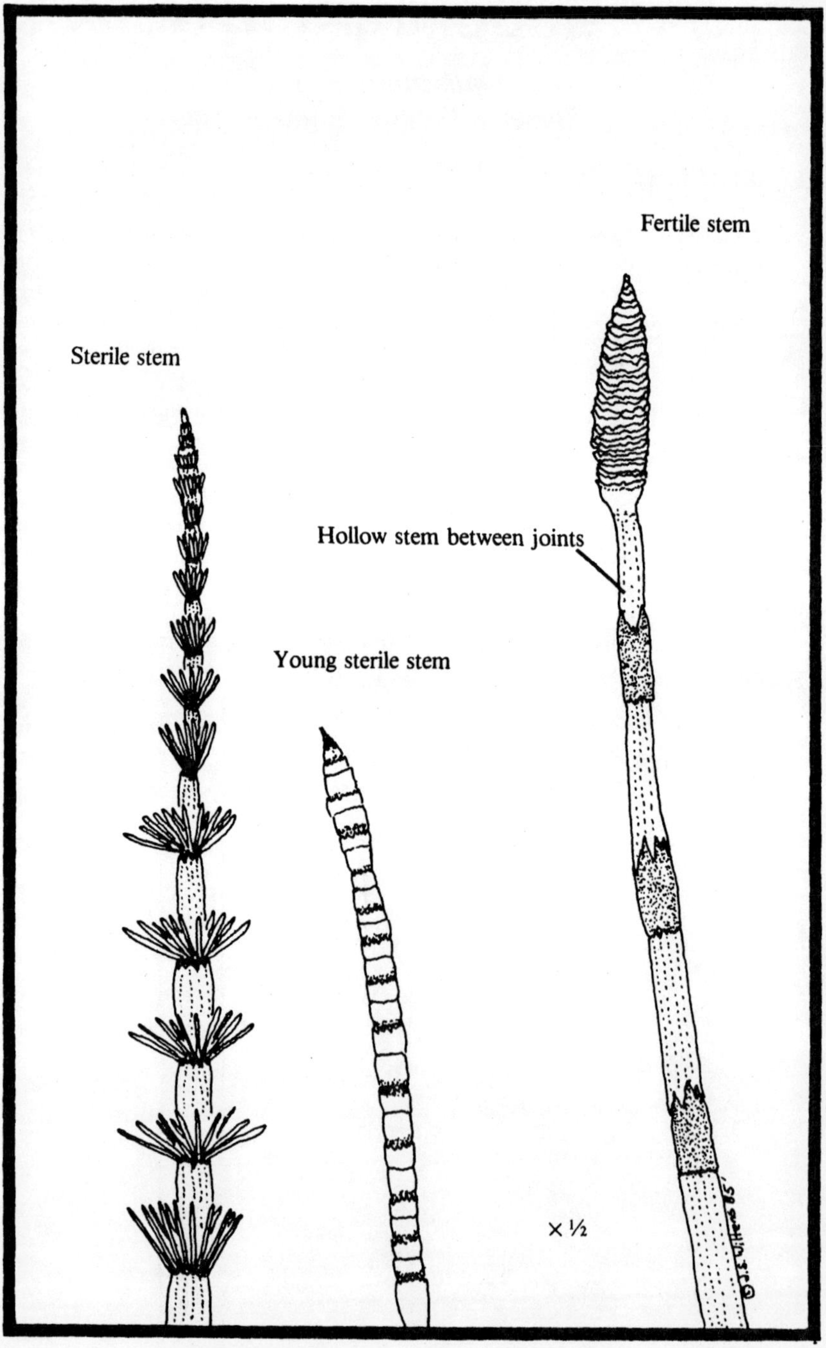

Scouring Rush (*Equisetum arvense*)

WILD CUCUMBER

Marah sps.
(Gourd Family: Cucurbitaceae)

OTHER NAMES: Big-Root, Chilicothe

DESCRIPTION: Vines are either trailing or climbing with the aid of corkscrew tendrils. The broad palmate leaves are borne alternately up the stem. The whitish green 5 petaled flowers are borne on a raceme (a raceme is an elongate axis which bears flowers on short stems in succession towards the apex). The fruit matures from a small fuzzy ball into a golf to baseball sized green sphere covered with green spines.

HABITAT: Open hillsides, empty lots, alongside trails. Often found trailing over other bushes.

CAUTION: ***The root is reputed to be edible, though quite bitter. Long boiling and frequent changes of water are necessary to make the root palatable. There is a suggestion that this plant is poisonous dependent on the amount of material consumed. Due to the questionable nature of this plant, it should be avoided.***

INTERESTING FACTS: The fruit may be dried and the spines removed to make a luffa, or scrubbing sponge.

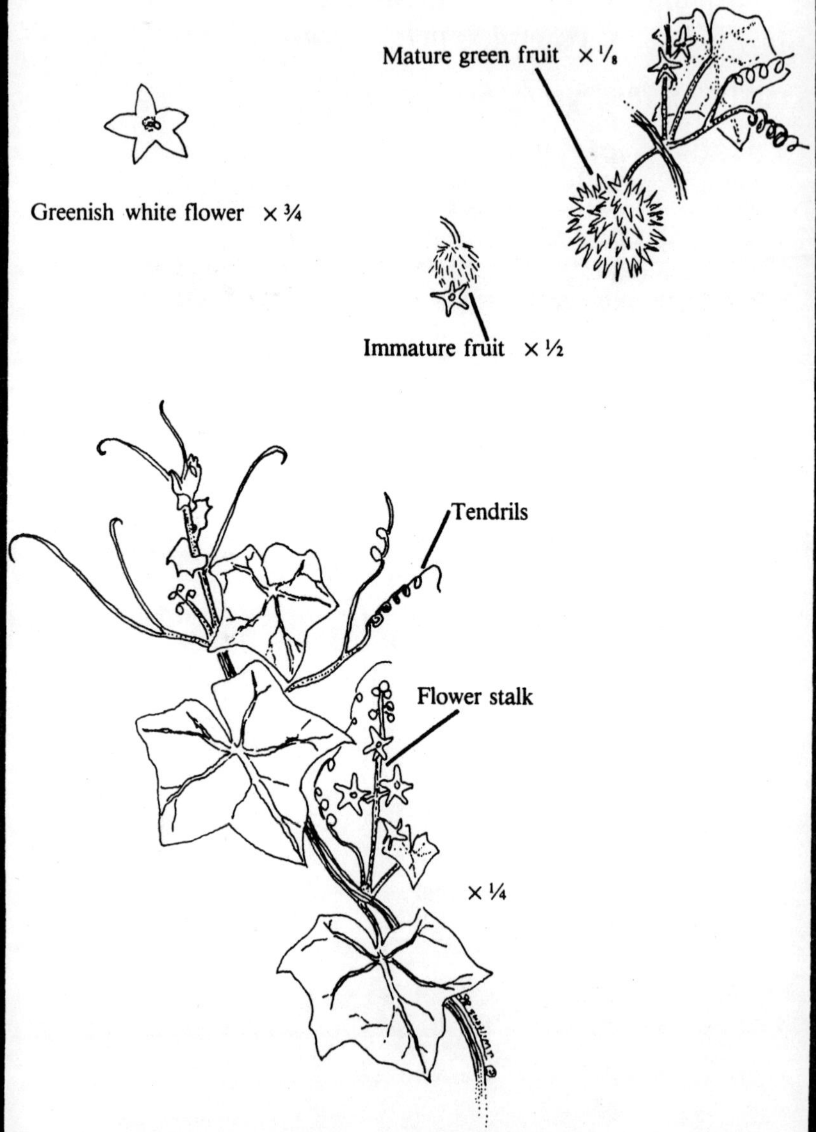

Wild Cucumber (*Marah sp.*)

BIBLIOGRAPHY

The following list comprises a portion of the research material surveyed by the author:

Balls, E.D. 1965. ***Early Uses of California Plants.*** University of California Press, Berkeley, California. 103 p.

Baker, H.G. 1965. ***Plants and Civilization.*** Wadsworth Publishing Company, Belmont, California. 183 p.

Bean, L.J., and Saubel, K.S. 1972. ***Temalpakh, Cahuilla Indian Knowledge and Usage of Plants.*** Malki Museum Press, Morongo Indian Reservation, Banning, California. 225 p.

Berglund, B., and Bolsby, C.E. 1977. ***The Complete Outdoorsman's Guide to Edible Wild Plants.*** Charles Scribner's Sons, New York. 189 p.

Callegari, J., and Durand, K. 1977. ***Wild Edible and Medicinal Plants of California.*** Published by Callegari and Durand, El Cerrito, California. 96 p.

Clark, D.E. 1979. ***Sunset New Western Garden Book.*** Lane Publishing Company, Menlo Park, California. 512 p.

Clarke, C.B. 1977. ***Edible and Useful Plants of California.*** University of California Press, Berkeley, California. 280 p.

Craighead, J.J., and Craighead, F.C., and Davis, R.J. 1963. ***A Field Guide to Rocky Mountain Wildflowers.*** The Riverside Press, Cambridge. 277 p.

Crowhurst, A. 1972. ***The Weed Cookbook.*** Lancer Books, New York. 190 p.

Domico, T. 1984. ***Wild Harvest.*** Hancock House Publishers, Blaine, Washington. 88 p.

Elias, S.T., and Dykeman, A.P. 1982. ***Field Guide to North American Edible Wild Plants.*** Outdoor Life Books, New York. 286 p.

Fielder, M. 1982. ***Fielder's Herbal Helper for Hunters, Trappers and Fisherman.*** Winchester Press, Tulsa, Oklahoma. 181 p.

Gibbons, E. 1962. ***Stalking the Wild Asparagus.*** David McKay Company, New York. 303 p.

Gibbons, E. 1966. ***Stalking the Healthful Herbs.*** David McKay Company, New York. 303 p.

Gilkey, H.M. 1957. ***Weeds of the Pacific Northwest.*** Oregon State College. 441 p.

Harrington, H.D., and Matsumura, Y. 1967. ***Western Wild Plants.*** The University of New Mexico Press, Albuquerque. 156 p.

Harris, B.C. 1971. ***Eat the Weeds.*** Barre Publishers, Massachusetts, 223 p.

Hutchens, A.R. 1973. ***Indian Herbalogy of North America.*** Merco, Ontario, Canada. 382 p.

James, W.R. 1973. ***Know Your Poisonous Plants.*** Naturegraph Publishers, Healdsburg, California. 99 p.

Kingsbury, J.M. 1964. ***Poisonous Plants of the United States and Canada.*** Prentice-Hall, Englewood Cliffs, New Jersey.

Kingsbury, J.M. 1965. ***Deadly Harvest.*** Holt, Rhinehart and Winston, New York. 128 p.

Kirk, D. 1970. ***Wild Edible Plants of the Western United States.*** Naturegraph Publishers, Healdsburg, California. 307 p.

Levy, C.K., and Primack, R.B. 1984. ***A Field Guide to Poisonous Plants and Mushrooms of North America.*** The Stephen Greene Press, Brattleboro, Vermont. 178 p.

Lewis, W.H., and Elvin-Lewis, M.P.F. 1977. ***Medical Botany.*** A Wiley Interscience Publication, New York. 515 p.

McPherson, A., and Mcpherson, S. 1979. ***Edible and Useful Wild Plants of the Urban West.*** Pruett Publishing Company, Boulder, Colorado. 330 p.

Muenscher, W.C. 1939. ***Poisonous Plants of the United States.*** The Macmillan Company, New York. 277 p.

Munz, A.M., and Keck, D.D. 1959. ***A California Flora.*** University of California Press, Berkeley and Los Angeles, California. 1681 p.

Niethammer, C. 1974. ***American Indian Food and Lore.*** Macmillan Publishing Company, New York. 191 p.

Nyerges, C., and Fryling, J. 1982. ***Guide to Wild Foods.*** Third Edition. Survival News Service, Los Angeles, California. 239 p.

Schulz, P.E. 1954. ***Indians of Lassen Volcanic Park and Vicinity.*** Loomis Museum Association, Mineral, California. 176 p.

Sturtevant, E.L. 1919. ***Sturtevant's Edible Plants of the World.*** Revised ed. 1972, editor Hedrick, U.P. Dover Publication, New York. 686 p.

Sweet, M. 1962. ***Common Edible and Useful Plants of the West.*** Naturegraph Company, Healdsburg, California. 64 p.

Weeden, N.F. 1986. ***A Sierra Nevada Flora.*** Wilderness Press, Berkeley, California. 406 p.

GLOSSARY

Axil: Upper angle formed by a leaf or branch with the stem.

Basal: Relating to, or situated at the base.

Bractlets: A reduced leaf borne on the stalk of a single flower in a flower cluster.

Elliptical: A flattened circle, more than twice as long as broad.

Lanceolate: Lance shaped; much longer than broad, tapering from below the middle to the tip and to the base.

Ovate: With the outline of a hen's egg in longitudinal section.

Palmate: Hand shaped with the fingers spread; in a leaf, having the lobes or divisions radiating from a common point.

Palmately compound: Having leaflets all arising from a single point.

Petiole: A leaf stalk.

Pinnate: A compound leaf, having the leaflets arranged on each side of a common petiole, featherlike.

Pinnatifid: Pinnately cleft into narrow lobes not reaching to the midrib.

Raceme: A simple, elongated indeterminate inflorescence, with each flower with its own flower stalk.

Rosette: A crowded cluster of radiating leaves appearing to arise from the ground.

Sepals: A usually green segment of the outer whorl of flower parts.

Spatulate: Like a spatula, a knife rounded above and gradually narrowed to the base.

Umbel: A flat or convex flower cluster in which the flower stalks arise from a common point, like rays of an umbrella.

ABOUT THE AUTHOR

"To a large extent I find my life has been guided by destiny. A destiny preconceived by a vocational test taken in high school. At the completion of this test I was told I had the disposition to be a scientist — or a farmer. The discrepancy between the two left me in dismay. A scientist or a farmer?

Well, I decided I certainly didn't want to be a farmer, so I had better get on the ball and work towards being a scientist.

And so I applied myself very diligently in high school. And after 4 years I graduated.

But I was told, by people who are knowledgeable about such things, that a high school diploma wasn't worth much in the real world. Strangely enough these 'explainers of the real world' were the very same people that had previously been so adamant about the importance of matriculating from high school.

But the 'authorities on such matters' convinced me. After all, did I want to end up being a 'farmer'? So with the threat of farmer in my subconscious, I enrolled at U.C. Berkeley.

And I studied very hard. And when it came time to declare my major, I found that I had become very fond of biology, specifically the section that dealt with botany. And so botany it was.

But, just before I graduated, I was told, by people who are knowledgeable about such things, that a B.A. was worthless in the real world. My real education could only be completed in graduate school.

And so, with a sense of **deja vu**, *I made plans to continue my education. To develop a strong foundation so that I would never have to become a farmer.*

After 3 more years I completed a brillant master's thesis, it must have been brilliant since the title is unintelligible to the bulk of the world 's population. And now I was surely ready to meet the real world.

But, low and behold, now I was told, by people who are knowledgeable about such things, that a Master's degree was really not worth anything in the real world. I would need to get a PHd. And so I applied and was accepted into a Doctorate program. But, as so often happens at crucial times, I had a personal revelation. A friend asked me if he should continue his education and live as a student pauper or enter the real world. Was he ready? My response was automatic, too automatic. "The real world," I replied, "but you only have one degree. You definitely need more schooling." Then a blasphemous thought entered my head, I did not really know the real world. And yet people were now considering me 'knowledgeable about such things'.

I had a decision: Academia, work force, work force, academia?

I had to know the truth. I cut the umbilical cord of academia. I would enter the work force. My first job was a research position in an isolated marine biology station in Canada, doing underseas research in aquaculture. Subsequently I moved to Hawaii, where I continued doing research in aquaculture. And it was here I had another revelation. After all these years of schooling, of struggling to be a scientist, I had gone full circle, I had ended up being an underwater 'FARMER'.

In addition to Jim's adventures in marine biology, he has been a university waterpolo coach of a nationally recognized Canadian team, a professional diver, an analytical chemist for firms in high tech Silicon Valley and a writer.

Jim presently devotes all his time to a very successful outdoor adventure school, Deer Crossing Wilderness Camp Inc. It is a special wilderness skills training facility, designed exclusively for teenagers.

Collecting wild plants has been part hobby and part avocation for Jim for many years. As Jim says, "*I even grow some of the weeds in my backyard, so I guess that makes me a wild 'farmer', there seems to be no escape.*"

DEER CROSSING CAMP INC.

The author wishes to thank Deer Crossing Wilderness Camp for its support in the publication of this book. Deer Crossing is a blend of wilderness school, adventure program and traditional camp values. It is a family owned operation with a unique philosophy. Increasingly teenagers need a respite from the hectic demands of technology and the pressure to 'grow up too fast'. Deer Crossing provides a program designed exclusively for the needs of teenagers. In a structured format it provides challenge and excellence of instruction, while instilling leadership qualities and a desire to excel.

Deer Crossing occupies a spectacular setting in the High Sierra. It is surrounded by a hundred square miles of National Forest, with an azure blue lake at it's front door. Base camp is a rustic lodge, providing a program of boardsailing, backpacking, martial arts, sailing, kayaking, canoeing, leadership training and more. At a time when many camps opt for quantity with 200 to 300 campers, Deer Crossing is dedicated to high quality and limits enrollment to 35 campers.

For information about this wonderful summer program, contact the San Francisco Bay Area Office of Deer Crossing Wilderness Camp, P.O. Box 831, Saratoga, CA 95071. Telephone: (408) 996-9448.

Printed in the United States
19925LVS00001B/457-462